Facilities and equipment

Activity sessions

Skills for employment

Index

Foreword

The Skills for Work courses are designed to allow you to experience the World of work. This may be achieved by you having access to realistic Sport and Recreation environments in a variety of both indoor and outdoor settings. You will also be encouraged to work with real clients and staff in these different realistic environments. This guide will help you prepare for this exciting, but challenging, World of Work as it prepares you to complete assessments in a realistic environment rather than conventional classroom settings.

This Success Guide covers each of the five mandatory units in the Intermediate 1 Sport & Recreation course. One topic area is addressed per double page spread to help you manage your progress through the course. While you are working through the course, it will allow you to gain an insight into what is involved when working in Sport and Recreation facilities, such as, leisure centres, outdoor centres, fitness gyms and swimming pools, etc.

This book aims to support that experience and reinforce your learning. Throughout the book, employability skills and self review sections will help you to develop good practice both within and away from the learning environment. This book also provides information on important Health & Safety legislation that you will be required to know for your course.

Bob Nielson
Qualifications Development Manager

Guide to symbols

	Whenever you see this symbol, it highlights where you will cover an employability skill. This is indicated by the number in its centre (see page 9 for a list of employability skills).
	These stars give you TOP TIPS on what you need to revise or learn on each page.
	At the end of each section there are QUICK TESTS to test your knowledge.

Skills for Work

Intermediate 1
Sport & Recreation

Emma Hayes

Contents

Introduction

Personal fitness

Accidents and emergencies

The course

Skills for Work courses are designed to help candidates acquire skills and knowledge in a particular subject.

In Skills for Work – Sport and Recreation (Intermediate 1), candidates will be supervised at all times by the 'person responsible' while they carry out a range of tasks in a sporting environment. These will be:

- **Personal fitness**
  Plan, implement and review your own fitness
- **Dealing with accidents and emergencies**
  Gain knowledge and understanding of a range of accidents and emergencies and following an organisation's procedures for dealing with these events
- **Dealing with facilities and equipment**
  Setting up, taking down and storing equipment; cleaning and tidying facility areas
- **Assisting with an activity session**
  Plan, assist and review activity sessions
- **Skills for employment**
  Customer interaction, good working relationships, review of own performance

Candidates will gain good foundation knowledge and learn basic skills in sport and recreation. This will give candidates a helping hand in furthering their career in this industry, whether they wish to continue in education or to gain employment.

The Skills for Work course will be delivered in a sport and-recreation environment. There is no set environment where the course can be delivered but here are some examples:

- sports hall,
- swimming pool,
- gym,
- outdoor centre,
- leisure centre.

The Units

There are five Units in the Skills for Work – Sport and Recreation (Intermediate 1) course. These Units are designed to give candidates a 'snapshot' of the different duties and activities that employees in the sport and recreation industry carry out on a daily basis.

As mentioned on page 5, the candidate will be assisting the person responsible at all times.

Personal fitness gives candidates the opportunity to learn about the components of fitness and to undertake a fitness test. They will then plan, organise and carry out their own physical training plan based on their initial test. Candidates will review their progress continuously and then draw up a revised physical training plan.

Accidents and emergencies introduces candidates to procedures for dealing with different types of accidents and emergencies. This Unit gives candidates a basic understanding of injuries and illnesses. It also highlights the role and responsibilities of candidates when dealing with any kind of emergency. The unit will cover the necessary health and safety issues relating to accidents and emergencies.

Facilities and equipment teaches candidates how activity equipment is set up, taken down and stored correctly according to centre and manufacturers' guidelines. Candidates will also learn how to clean and tidy facility areas and the importance of following health and safety guidelines for cleaning materials and equipment.

Activity sessions allow candidates to learn what goes into the planning of an activity, and what equipment they need before they assist with the activity. Candidates will be expected to assist the person responsible with client reviews and a review of their own performance.

Skills for employment covers aspects of good customer care. Candidates will learn how to greet customers appropriately, assist with their needs to the best of their ability, and meet the centre/organisation's standards for appearance and behaviour. Candidates will have to ensure that they maintain good working relationships with others and review their own performance, looking at their strengths and weaknesses and identifying action points.

Training and assessment

This book refers throughout to the '**person responsible**'. This person is someone who has direct responsibility for the assigned task and is in a supervisory capacity over the candidate – for example, a teacher/tutor or a coach/instructor.

Most of the Units are designed to be assessed not in a classroom setting but in a '**realistic working environment**'. A realistic environment is one that allows candidates access to sport-and-recreation equipment, facilities and clients (customer/users) – for example, a leisure centre, swimming pool, outdoor centre or fitness suite. The Units allow for some of candidates' **training** to be carried out in a **classroom setting** for example, the Knowledge and Understanding aspects of dealing with accidents and emergencies, but the **assessments** will be carried out in a '**realistic working environment**'.

The Units in the course are designed to be integrated with each other. An example of this is:

- **Facilities and equipment** and **Activity sessions**: Setting up equipment, carrying out an activity session, taking down and storing equipment after use.

Candidates are assessed using a variety of methods, including:

- practical scenarios;
- observation;
- Knowledge and Understanding set questions;
- set assessment papers, such as activity session plans, or accident/emergency reports;
- candidate log sheets.

Employability skills

A key feature of the Skills for Work course are the 'employability skills' that are built into the course. Through undertaking a range of activities and tasks candidates work to develop particular skills that are needed in the sport-and-recreation industry. These skills are seen by employers as necessary for carrying out a variety of jobs in a centre or organisation.

On the opposite page is a table that lists all the employability skills on which candidates will be assessed. During their training, candidates will focus on specific employability skills in relation to a particular subject – for example, employability skill number 9: Timekeeping. Most candidates have had experience in timekeeping:

- being on time for a bus;
- being on time to meet friends.

In each Unit, candidates are given the opportunity to review their employability skills with the person responsible. Candidates have to rate their performance (1 = being very good at that skill/attitude, 5 = being poor) against a list of employability skills that are specific to the Unit they are working on. The person responsible is allowed to give their own rating before reviewing candidates' performance and listing action points for future training and development.

Employability skills

This table shows the employability skills that will be assessed in the Units of the Skills for Work – Sport and Recreation course. In the first column are all the employability skills. The second column signposts the Units in which these can be found.

A = Personal fitness

B = Accidents and emergencies

C = Facilities and equipment

D = Activity sessions

E = Skills for employment

Employability skills	Assessed in Unit
1. Reviewing progress/reviewing	A, B, E
2. Dealing with customers/customer care	A, B
3. Taking advice/taking advice from others	A, B, C, E
4. Self-assessment	A, E
5. Setting targets	A, B, E
6. Wearing appropriate dress	A, B, C
7. Working cooperatively/working cooperatively with others	A, D
8. Planning and preparation	B, E
9. Timekeeping	B
10. Giving advice	B
11. Completing tasks	B
12. Awareness of health and safety procedures	C, D
13. Following instructions	C, D
14. Time management	E

Throughout this book you will be able to see which employability skills have been covered by the following symbol.

The number featured in the whistle indicates which employability skill has been covered.

Health and safety

Basic health and safety issues

Candidates must be aware of **basic health and safety** issues.

Candidates will take part in some form of induction to the course in the **realistic working environment** where they will be carrying out their tasks.

Each Unit will have its own specific health and safety issues, for example:

Activity sessions:

- specific activity and equipment safety,
- participant safety,
- risk assessing.

Facilities and equipment:

- control of Substances,
- personal Protective Equipment,
- manual handling.

Accidents and emergencies:

- health and hygiene,
- personal Protective Equipment,
- personal safety and caring for casualties in emergencies.

Your role

The Skills for Work course allows candidates to learn through experience. It is important to understand what kind of role you will play. You will assist the person responsible at all times – at no point will you be allowed to take charge of an activity or task.

Sport and recreation contacts

For further information and reading:

Organisation name	Scottish Qualifications Authority	SkillsActive
Address	The Optima Building 58 Robertson Street Glasgow G2 8DQ	Castlewood House 77–91 New Oxford Street London WC1A 1PX
Telephone number	0845 279 1000	020 7632 2000
Website Address	www.sqa.org.uk	www.skillsactive.com
Who are they?	The qualifications authority for Scotland	The Sector Skills Council for Sport and Recreation
Organisation Name	Scottish Further Education Unit	Health and Safety Executive
Address	Argyll Court Castle Business Park Stirling FK9 4TY	HSE Infoline Caerphilly Business Park Caerphilly, CF83 3GG
Telephone Number	01786 892000	0845 345 0055
Website Address	www.sfeu.ac.uk	www.hse.gov.uk
Who are they?	SFEU is the key development agency for Scotland's colleges	Responsible for health and safety regulation in Great Britain

Other useful contacts:		
	First aid	STA – www.sta.co.uk BASP – www.basp.org.uk Red Cross – www.redcross.org.uk St. John's Ambulance – www.sja.org.uk
	Coaching	Sports leaders – www.bst.org.uk Sportscotland – www.sportscotland.org.uk BWLA – www.bwla.co.uk Lifesavers – www.lifesafers.org.uk
	Other health and safety	BICSc – www.bics.org.uk Child protection – www.childprotectioninsport.co.uk Data protection – http://www.opsi.gov.uk/ACTS/acts1998/19980029.htm

Personal fitness

This Unit is designed for you to learn the basics of fitness. It is important that, while you are undertaking your fitness tests and training, it is done under the supervision of the **person responsible** at all times.

With the assistance of the person responsible, you will learn about:

- the relevant health-and-safety factors related to carrying out personal fitness
- how to warm up before and cool down after you carry out exercise
- what the different components of fitness are and how to go about carrying out a fitness baseline test
- how baseline fitness tests are carried out
- how to record results and take part in monitoring of your physical training plan
- how to review your progress with the person responsible.

With the person responsible, you will be planning and organising your own physical training plan before carrying it out over a period of time. To assist you with developing a physical training plan, you will undertake baseline tests of various components of fitness. Based on these results, your physical training plan will then be drawn up.

Over this time, you will be expected to record the training you are undertaking, monitor it and review it at regular intervals as agreed with the person responsible.

With the assistance of the person responsible, you will be expected to demonstrate the following when you are developing your physical training plan:

- importance of an ongoing personal physical training plan and how this links to areas in sport and recreation
- carrying out your physical training in an appropriate sport-and-recreation environment with a range of appropriate equipment and facilities
- identifying appropriate goals (short and long term) for your fitness
- identifying health-and-safety considerations
- reviewing the physical training plan with the person responsible before putting it into operation and setting review dates.

As you are carrying out your physical training plan, you will be expected to record your results of any training that you have completed, and at regular intervals you will evaluate this physical training plan and make the appropriate revisions to help you achieve your goal.

At the end of your physical training period, you will be expected to present evidence of your progress for a review with the person responsible. This will consist of a review of areas of your physical training that went well and areas that need to be improved, a second baseline fitness test, drawing up a modified physical training plan for your future developments and modifying a plan for future personal fitness development.

What employability skills are in this section?

In this section you will have the opportunity to develop a range of **employability skills**. These are:

1 Reviewing progress

3 Taking advice from others

4 Self-assessment

5 Setting targets

8 Planning and preparation

14 Time management

T🌞p Tip
Remember, any words in GREEN are explained in the GLOSSARY section on pages 92 and 93.

T🌞p Tip
Look out for the symbol to see where the **employability skills** have been covered.

Health and safety for personal fitness

Health and safety checklist

It is vital that you consider basic health and safety when you carry out any fitness programs. Ensure that you do the following:

- make sure you are supervised by the **person responsible** when carrying out your training;
- do not eat a large meal before exercising and keep hydrated at all times;
- be fit and well enough to carry out physical exercise;
- wear **appropriate clothing and footwear;**
- warm up before doing any training and cool down after you have finished;
- **follow the manufacturer's guidelines** when using fitness equipment and ensure that it is in good working condition before using it;
- if you are using a fitness facility conduct yourself in an appropriate manner;
- be aware of your safety if you are not using a fitness facility – for example, when road running.

Top Tip

It is important that you learn the basic health-and-safety considerations for your personal training plan.

Quick Test

1 Who should supervise you when you train?

2 What must you wear when carrying out any training?

3 What must you do when using fitness equipment?

4 What must you be aware of if you are not using a fitness facility?

Answers 1 The person responsible. **2** Appropriate clothing and footwear. **3** Follow the manufacturer's guidelines. **4** Your safety.

Warming up and cooling down

What is it, and why do we do it?

Warming up takes place before you exercise. Warming up reduces the risk of injury and prepares your body for the exercise session.

Warm-ups generally include **cardio-respiratory exercise** (exercise that involves the heart and lungs), which gradually increases to allow the body to warm up, and mobility or **stretching exercises** to prepare the body further for vigorous exercise.

Cooling down takes place after you have finished your exercise session. It reduces the risk of muscle soreness or injury, and brings the body gradually back to normal.

Cooling down generally includes **cardio-respiratory exercise**, which decreases to cool the body down, and **stretching and relaxation exercises** to bring the body back to a steady state.

You should try to warm up and cool down the muscles most appropriate for the activity you will be taking part in. The main differences between warm-up and cool-down activities are the length of time taken and the intensity of activity involved. Examples of these exercises for sporting activities include:

- Swimmers: several leisurely laps of the pool.
- Footballers: shorter sprints at a slower speed.
- Runners: beginning the run at a slower speed.
- Tennis: hitting the ball back and forth to the other player.

Top Tip
Always get help from the person responsible to devise your warm up and cool down exercises.

Quick Test

1 Can you name two different types of warm-up exercise?

2 Can you name two different types of cool-down exercise?

3 Give an example of a sport and a warm-up exercise.

4 Give an example of a sport and a cool-down exercise.

Answers 1 Cardio-respiratory and stretching. 2 Cardio-respiratory and stretching and relaxation. 3 Any one of the bulleted list. 4 Any one of the bulleted list.

Different methods of training

Approaches

There are a number of ways you can train for each of the components of fitness. It is important that you work with the person responsible to establish what tests you should do. Below are examples of the most common areas explored in a baseline fitness test.

Strength

Resistance training: using a range of **free or fixed weights**; carrying out low resistance and/or repetition – for example, going to the gym.

Top Tip
You will be tested on one or more of these components of fitness when you carry out your baseline fitness assessment.

Cardio-respiratory

Activities that keep your heart rate elevated at a safe level for a sustained length of time. Walking, swimming and cycling are all cardio-respiratory exercises. Start off slowly, and gradually work up to a more intense pace.

Flexibility

Sit and reach for your toes. This simple test will measure the mobility of your hamstring (the muscle at the back of your upper leg) and lower back.

Muscle endurance

Series of exercises that target certain parts of the body – for example, **press-ups**, **sit-ups**, **weight training**. Use high repetition when carrying out these types of exercises. Use low weights with high repetition.

Speed

Timed sprints: sprint running over a set distance, for example, 20 metres.

Quick Test

1 What kind of activity focuses on the heart and lungs?

2 What kind of activity focuses on the range of mobility?

3 What kind of activities would you take part in for muscle endurance training?

4 What kind of activities would you take part in for strength training?

Answers 1 Cardio-respiratory. 2 Flexibility. 3 Press-ups, sit-ups, weight training. 4 Free or fixed weights.

Components of fitness

Improving your fitness

When you want to improve your fitness, you should train in one or more of the components of fitness. The components are: strength, power, agility, balance, cardio-respiratory, flexibility, local muscle endurance and speed. These individual components will help you to improve your overall fitness, which will improve your performance in sporting activities.

What are the components of fitness?

Strength

The greatest force a muscle or muscle group can produce. To improve your **strength** try bodyweight activities, lifting weights and using resistance bands/tubes.

Power

Great force of strength and speed in an explosive burst. To improve your **power** try jumping or sprint starting.

Agility

The ability to carry out a series of power movements quickly in different directions, for example, zigzag running.

Balance

The ability to control the body's position in a stationary position or while moving, for example, a handstand or gymnastic movement.

Cardio-respiratory

The ability of the heart to deliver blood to working muscles over a period of time and the ability of the lungs to deliver oxygen to working muscles via the blood supply. To improve your cardio-respiratory fitness try swimming, running or walking.

Flexibility

The ability to extend the range of motion around a joint or group of joints. To improve your **flexibility** try touching your toes or swimming.

Local muscle endurance

The ability of a muscle or muscle group to exert force during an activity and to perform over a long period of time. To improve your **local muscle endurance** try rowing, lifting weights or quickly walking/running up stairs.

Speed

The ability to perform a movement in a short period of time. To improve your **speed** try running or swimming at a higher speed.

Top Tip
Make sure you understand what the components of fitness are.

Baseline fitness

What is your fitness baseline?

Before taking part in any fitness training, it is important to check what your baseline fitness is.

With assistance from the person responsible, you will carry out different exercises that cover the components of fitness, for example: strength, muscular endurance, flexibility and cardio-respiratory. The type of activities you take part in will be agreed beforehand with the person responsible and could be different from the examples given below.

Top Tip
Make sure you know what a fitness baseline is!

Examples of the exercises you could be taking part in are:

Strength

Resistance training.

Exercising using a range of fixed weights.

High weights, used at low repetition, with a long rest in between each set of repetitions.

Flexibility

Static stretching.

Stretching and holding the body in a full range of movement.

Stretching the body, holding the body in position for 30 seconds and then progressing.

Muscular endurance

Circuit training.

Series of different exercises that target different parts of the body.

Approx. eight stations, exercise for 45 seconds at each, resting 30 seconds in between each exercise.

Cardio-respiratory

Continuous.

Working at the same pace over a period of time.

Ten minute cycle at 60rpm.

Recording your results

After you have completed your fitness baseline tests, it is vital that you record your results. You need to write down:

- the date of the test;
- the component of fitness you were tested against;
- the name of the kind of test that was carried out;
- the result of your test.

Date	Component of fitness	Name of test	Results
1/5/07	Flexibility	Sit and reach	+1
1/5/07	Cardio-respiratory	Leger test (bleep)	4.0

Why record your results?

Record your results will allow you to:

- find out your current level of fitness;
- find out what components of fitness you need to improve;
- find out what components of fitness you are best at;
- compare your results with friends and others who are your age and gender;
- establish how to proceed with your training plan.

Top Tip
Make sure you know how to record the results of your fitness baseline test.

Quick Test

1 Name a baseline fitness exercise for muscular endurance.

2 Name an example of a flexibility exercise.

3 Who will you be working with to carry out your baseline fitness test?

4 Name two pieces of information you need to record for your baseline fitness test.

Answers 1 Circuit training. 2 Static stretching. 3 The person responsible. 4 Date, component of fitness, name of test, results.

Planning a physical training plan

First steps

You will plan and organise your own physical training plan with the help of the person responsible. By now, you will have taken part in your baseline fitness test and recorded your results. The next step is to analyse your results and find out what areas of your fitness need to be improved upon. This will form the basis of your physical training plan.

Your **physical training plan** will consist of:

- baseline fitness results,
- physical training plan objectives,
- what warm-up exercises you will be taking part in,
- your work-out schedule,
- what cool-down exercises you will be taking part in,
- short and long-term goals.

Top Tip

It is important when you carry out your physical training that all health and safety issues are dealt with (see page 14) and that you do not stray from what was discussed and agreed with the person responsible.

Be SMART!

When you are planning and organising your physical training plan, it is important that any goals you set are SMART.

Specific   State the outcome you want clearly.

Measurable   Know when you've achieved your goals.

Attainable   Ensure it is possible to achieve your goals.

Realistic   Ensure you have realistic goals.

Time-phased   Set a deadline for achieving your goals.

Carrying out your physical training

At this stage, you should have a clear understanding of which areas of your fitness you need to focus on.

Draw up a timetable of how you will carry out your physical training, the best time to carry out your training and how you will record what training you have done.

Candidate's name: Jim Hall	Activity/task: Fitness programme: flexibility
Date	Personal fitness log details
3rd May	Venue: Sports hall
	Details: Carried out static stretching exercises, focusing on lower body before I went on a cycle ride

Your physical training should take place on a regular basis, for example twice a week, and it should be based on the baseline fitness test you completed earlier. Targets and goals will be set for you to complete over both short and longer periods of time.

It is important that you record your training as accurately as possible. This is usually noted down in a **diary or log book** and it will allow you to follow your training programme all the way through to your final evaluation.

Top Tip
Make sure you record what you do during each session of physical training.

Quick Test

1 What does the 'R' in SMART mean?

2 Name three features of a physical training plan.

3 What do you record your training in?

4 Who will help you to draw up your physical training plan?

Answers **1** Realistic. **2** Name three out of the bulleted list on page 20. **3** Diary or log book. **4** The person responsible.

Evaluating your plan

Measuring progress

Evaluations will be carried out throughout your personal fitness training.

With the **person responsible**, you will look at your baseline fitness test and fitness log to see whether you are progressing. After this evaluation your physical training plan may remain the same or be altered.

If your initial physical training plan is altered, this may be because:

- You have reached your goal in a specific component of fitness
- The targets set may have been too easy for you to achieve
- You may be struggling in the targets set
- You may have suffered an injury
- The facilities you were using may not be available any more

Once your evaluation is complete, you should continue to carry out your physical fitness plan until the end of the period that has been set.

Top Tip
Don't forget to continue completing the personal fitness log!

Retesting baseline fitness

Once you have completed your fitness training programme you will be expected to take part in a retest of your baseline fitness.

It is important that you take part in the **same activities** under the **same conditions**, against the **same components** of fitness as your initial test so that you can see if you have improved and reached your goals.

Top Tip
Don't be disheartened if you have not progressed as much as you want. Some activities or exercises take a little longer than others to have an effect..

Date	Component of fitness	Name of test	Results
1/7/07	Flexibility	Sit and reach	+1.5
1/7/07	Cardio-respiratory	Leger test (bleep)	5.0

Why do we test the same components and activities?

This is to ensure that you can see where improvements have been made. For example, if you wanted to improve your flexibility for a specific activity such as gymnastics, you would not be taking part in strength training (using a range of fixed weights).

Why the same conditions?

This is to ensure that you are fairly tested. For example, when carrying out a Leger test:

- the test **would not** be valid if you were tested in a gym hall and then retested outside when it was windy and rainy;
- the test **would** be valid if the initial test and the retest took place in the gym hall.

 Quick Test

1 With whom will you evaluate your baseline fitness test?

2 When will you retest your baseline fitness?

3 Would you carry out a retest of your baseline fitness with different components of fitness from your initial test?

4 Would you carry out your retest under different conditions?

Answers 1 The person responsible. 2 Once you have completed your fitness training programme. 3 No. 4 No.

Training plan review

Collecting information

At the **end of your physical training**, it is important to collect as much information as possible about what you have been doing.

The types of information you need to collect are:

- the initial aims of your fitness training;
- your initial baseline fitness test results;
- your training plan and training log;
- your baseline fitness retest results.

At the end of your physical training period, you will need to present this information to **the person responsible** to carry out a review of your physical training. The person responsible will look at all the information presented and analyse the results of your initial baseline fitness test, your period of training and your second baseline fitness test. At the end of the review process, a modified training plan will be drawn up for future physical training.

Identifying improvements to the training plan

When you undergo a review of your physical training you will be looking at:

- how you have performed over the period of time since you took the initial fitness baseline test;
- what your short and long-term goals were in the beginning;
- your completed training log;
- your baseline fitness retest.

Once you have discussed with the person responsible how well your personal fitness training went, it is important to **discuss aspects of the plan that could be changed or improved** to suit any future training.

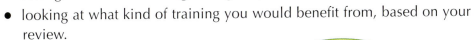

Drawing up a modified physical training plan

Once the review has taken place you will be asked to draw up **a modified training plan**.

This could involve:

- setting new short and long-term goals;
- looking at what kind of training you would benefit from, based on your review.

Get out and do!

✎ Quick Test

1 When do you collect information for your review?

2 Who will you need to present this information to?

3 What could you discuss with the person responsible?

4 What will you draw up when the review has taken place?

Dealing with accidents and emergencies

What to do

This Unit is designed to teach you about the different types of accidents and emergencies you may encounter in a sport-and-recreation environment and how to deal with them according to the centre or organisation's policies and procedures.

Your tutor will describe the signs and symptoms of the most common illnesses and injuries. You will also learn about different types of emergencies, for example fire and theft. By taking part in practical scenarios, you will gain further knowledge and experience about what to do in these situations. Your instructor will explain the definitions and treatments of injuries, illnesses and emergencies in greater detail.

You will be expected to demonstrate knowledge and understanding of procedures related to accidents and emergencies. This will involve identifying the correct centre/organisational procedures to follow, and being able to identify specific procedures. These will include:

+ following the relevant health-and-safety guidelines;
+ carrying out your responsibilities in an accident situation;
+ completing the relevant reports (accident and emergency).

For both accidents and emergencies you will have to participate in situations which will allow you to demonstrate that you can respond to an accident or emergency safely, can follow the instructions of the person responsible, and can follow the centre/organisation's guidelines at all times.

What employability skills are in this Unit?

In this Unit you will have the opportunity to develop a range of employability skills. These are:

 working cooperatively/working cooperatively with others;

 awareness of health and safety procedures;

 following instructions.

Top Tip
Look out for the symbol to see where the **employability skills** have been covered.

Top Tip
Remember, any words in GREEN are explained in the GLOSSARY section on pages 92 and 93.

Roles and responsibilities

In an accident or emergency situation it is very important that you abide by the roles and responsibilities laid down by the organisation or centre. All centres have a set of 'do's and don'ts' that staff must follow. Basic health and safety requirements determine how many first-aid kits and first-aiders are needed and staff and clients need to be made aware of where in the centre/organisation they can get first aid treatment.

When dealing with **injuries and illnesses**, make sure that you follow the following **procedures**:

+ **assess the area:** make sure you check whether it is safe to approach a casualty – you don't want to become a casualty yourself!

+ **get help!** Find the person responsible and follow their instructions;

+ **wear personal protective equipment:** put on the correct equipment as instructed by the person responsible.

When dealing with **emergencies**, the following **procedures** will have to be applied:

+ **assess the area:** make sure you check whether it is safe to approach the emergency – you don't want to become a casualty yourself!

+ **get help!** Find the person responsible and follow their instructions;

+ **DO NOT deal** with any security or fire issues yourself, no matter how minor the incident!

Organisational policies

Procedures and policies

All organisations will have **procedures** and **policies** that cover **first-aid and emergencies**. This is a **process** that ensures that the organisation has:

+ identified what **hazards** are in the centre/organisation;
+ thought about the kinds of emergencies that could happen and their **consequences**;
+ assessed the **likelihood** of something happening;
+ identified steps to **reduce this risk**.

These processes are called a risk assessment. A risk assessment is used to set guidelines for the general running of a centre, for clients using the centre while on activities, and for what actions to take in an emergency. These sets of guidelines are known as the NOP and the EAP.

The NOP and the EAP

These procedure documents are usually called the **N**ormal **O**perating **P**lan (**NOP**) and the **E**mergency **A**ction **P**lan (**EAP**). It is the responsibility of the organisation to ensure that:

+ these documents are up to date and revised regularly;
+ all staff have read and understood the content;
+ all staff carry out their duties according to the predetermined policies;
+ appropriate action is taken where staff do not abide by the policies.

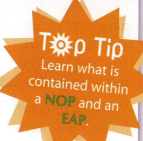

Top Tip
Learn what is contained within a NOP and an EAP.

As a health and safety requirement, all members of staff must keep themselves up to date with new procedures and must ensure that they carry out their duties safely.

Normal Operating Plan (NOP)

The **NOP** is a detailed day-to-day procedure document which has to be followed by all staff. Here is an example of the content of a **NOP**.

+ An outline of all the known **hazards** and sport specific-hazards in the organisation – for example, a swimming pool. This would also include risk assessments.

+ Sport-specific rules and regulations for customers and staff – for example, rules for the use of fitness suites, or wearing uniforms.

+ Staff duties and responsibilities.

+ Admissions policy and customer interaction – for example, how to communicate appropriately with customers.

+ Guidelines to deal with customers or staff who do not abide by the policies.

+ Policies on video or photographic equipment.

+ Training and development plans.

+ Health-and-safety: personal protective equipment (PPE), first aid.

+ Operational systems and systems of work and emergencies.

+ Alarms and safety equipment – for example, whistles, throw lines and so on.

Emergency Action Plan (EAP)

The **EAP** is a detailed description of procedures that all members of staff must follow in the event of an emergency. Here is an example of the content of an **EAP**:

+ Procedures for dealing with minor and major emergencies.

+ Sport specific injuries and illnesses – for example, canoeing accidents, or the use of spinal boards.

+ Roles and responsibilities of staff, organisation's first-aiders and medical assistance.

+ Other types of emergencies – for example, fire.

Top Tip
Ask the person responsible for a copy of the NOP and the EAP for you to have a look through.

Quick Test

1 What must all organisations have in place that covers first aid?

2 Whose responsibility is it that NOPs and EAPs are kept up to date?

3 What does NOP stand for?

4 What does EAP stand for?

Answers 1 Procedures and policies. 2 The organisation's. 3 Normal Operating Plan. 4 Emergency Action Plan.

Health, safety and personal protective equipment

Safety first!

In any **accident or emergency situation**, **health and safety** is very important. You have to ensure the safety of **yourself** above **anyone else**, no matter how bad the situation.

Before you go rushing into a situation, think about the following points.

+ **Find out about the incident and inform the person responsible:** the more information you have the better. You can then pass on this information to the person responsible, who will then make a decision on what action to take.

+ **Assess the scene:** look around you and see whether it is safe to continue.

+ **Report back to the person responsible:** in any situation it is important that you report back to the correct person. Where a major incident has taken place, such as a fire, organisations will have a procedure which all staff must follow – for example, not talking to the press or publicising casualty information.

+ **Wearing correct personal protective equipment (PPE):** all staff must wear PPE to ensure that they do not harm themselves while carrying out duties in emergencies – for example, first-aid gloves.

Top Tip
It is important that you carry out your duties to the ability you are trained in at all times.

Accident and emergency reports

No matter how small an incident, it must be reported. Whether it be an accident or an emergency, **report** forms are used to keep a record of the history of incidents and to see if there is an accident trend. This information can be called upon as evidence in court.

An accident report form

This form is used to report incidents of **near miss, injury, physical violence, verbal abuse, dangerous occurrences and notifiable diseases**.

An emergency report form

This form is used to report incidents of **fire, security or other types of emergencies**.

It is important that all reports are stored in a safe location and comply with the **Data Protection Act**.

Top Tip
Make sure you know how to complete an accident report form.

Quick Test

1 Whose safety must you ensure in an incident?

2 Why would you assess the scene of an incident?

3 What form would you need to complete if someone was injured?

4 What form would you complete if there was a security incident?

Injuries

What is a minor injury?

A minor injury is one where **treatment can be administered by a first-aider (the person responsible)**. All organisations will have first-aiders on site who are appropriately qualified. For example, an outdoor instructor will be trained in how to deal with casualties specifically in the outdoors, as will a pool lifeguard with situations relating to water. These may be the only people who deal with first aid in the centre or organisation; or first-aiding may be only one part of their work duty.

It is important to note that, in some cases, a minor injury may need medical assistance to confirm that the casualty has no other injuries – for example, a child with a sprained ankle could also have a broken bone in their ankle.

Minor injuries can happen at any time or in any place and can range from a grazed knee to getting sunburned. The table below shows types of minor injuries and examples of each:

Injury	Examples
Wound	Bruise, graze, cuts
Sprains and strains	Ankle, knee, wrist, elbow and so on
Burns and scalds	Sunburn, chemical, hot water, steam and so on
Eyes	Eyelash or dirt in eye
Breathing difficulties	Choking on food or drink

If a client comes up to you with a minor injury, or you have to deal with a minor injury, it is important that you follow the same procedures at all times.

+ Assess the area for any danger.

+ Reassure the casualty.

+ Take the casualty to the person responsible (first-aider).

OR

+ Go and get the person responsible to deal with the casualty.

+ Follow all the instructions given to you by the person responsible.

Top Tip
Something to consider: any minor injury <u>CAN</u> turn into a <u>MAJOR</u> injury.

Top Tip
Wear PPE at all times.

What is a major injury?

A major injury is one where **treatment must be given by paramedics or doctors**. Although first-aiders will be the people who will be with the casualty first to assess their injuries, they cannot give any medication for pain relief or set broken bones, for example, so the casualty WILL need to be treated by professional medics in a hospital.

Major injuries are different from minor injuries. This is because these types of injuries can be potentially life-threatening and immediate action needs to be taken to prevent the injury from worsening.

The table below shows types of major injuries and examples of each.

Injury (major)	Examples
Wound	Deep cuts, puncture wound (knife)
Sprains and strains	Ankle, knee, wrist, elbow
Burns and scalds	Sunburn, chemical, hot water
Eyes	Eyelash, dirt, objects embedded in the eye
Breathing difficulties	Choking on food or drink can lead to the casualty not breathing
Fractures	Broken bones

If you have been informed of someone who has a major injury, or you have to deal with a major injury, it is important that you follow the same procedures at all times.

+ Assess the area for danger.
+ Reassure the casualty.
+ Go and get the person responsible to deal with the casualty.
+ Follow all the instructions given to you by the person responsible.

Top Tip
NEVER give a casualty food or drink!

Quick Test

1 What is a minor injury?

2 What is a major injury?

3 Who should you contact if someone has sustained an injury?

4 What makes a major injury different from a minor injury?

Answers 1 Treatment can be administered by a first-aider. 2 Treatment must be administered by professional medical assistance. 3 The person responsible. 4 Major injuries can be potentially life-threatening.

Illnesses

What is a minor illness?

A minor illness is one where the casualty usually has a history of the illness, although in not in all cases. **The first-aider (the person responsible) should be able to deal with any minor illness** and if necessary will know when to seek professional medical assistance.

Examples of minor illnesses and definitions.

Illness (minor)	Definitions
Asthma	Breathing difficulties – casualties usually carry inhalers
Diabetes	Body cannot regulate its sugar production – casualties will carry testing kits and sugary food
Epilepsy	Electrical disturbance in the brain – casualties may seem to be daydreaming
Allergic reactions	Insect stings, food etc, – casualties may break out in a rash, have difficulty in breathing (depending on where the reaction is)
Hypothermia (cold)	Casualty's core temperature has dropped – casualty will be shivering, unable to get warm
Hyperthermia (hot)	Casualty's core temperature has risen – casualty will be sweating and have a 'red', flushed face
Poisoning	Through drinking, injecting, breathing etc. Look for possible causes i.e. bottle of bleach, and give this to the medical assistance
Water inhalation	Breathed in water: coughing up water – get medical assistance
Head injuries	Trauma to the head – fracture, illness – may feel dizzy, sick, have a headache

Top Tip
NEVER give a casualty any medication – allow them to administer it themselves.

What is a major illness?

A major illness is where the casualty has a past history (not in all cases) of the illness and **needs immediate medical assistance**. The role of the person responsible (who will be the first-aider) will be to make the casualty as comfortable as possible and carry out treatment until professional medical assistance arrives.

Examples of major illnesses and definitions.

Illness (major)	Definitions
Asthma	Breathing difficulties - casualties usually carry inhalers, but may go unconscious due to lack of oxygen
Diabetes	Body cannot regulate its sugar production - casualties will carry testing kits and sugary food; may become unconscious
Epilepsy	Electrical disturbance in the brain - casualties will have 'fits' and then they will sleep soundly
Allergic reactions	Insect stings, food and so on - casualties may have difficulty breathing and may become unconscious
Stroke	Blood vessels in the brain get blocked - the casualty may 'droop' down one side and be weak on that same side
Hypothermia (cold)	Casualty's core temperature has dropped - casualty will NOT be shivering; lack of coordination, collapsing, unconsciousness
Hyperthermia (hot)	Casualty's core temperature has risen - casualty will NOT be sweating and have a red, flushed face; feeling sick and confused, unconscious
Poisoning	Through drinking, injecting, breathing and so on. Look for possible causes (e.g. bottle of bleach), and give this to the professional medical assistance
Shock	Body begins to shut down when it has suffered a major injury or illness
Heart problems	Angina, heart attack - tightness around the chest, in pain, may go into shock
Water inhalation	Drowning - fighting for air, panicking, may become unconscious

Top Tip
If the casualty has any medication, allow THE CASUALTY to take it themselves.

Quick Test

1 What is a minor illness?

2 What is a major illness?

3 If a casualty has medication for their illness, what must you do?

4 What is shock?

Unconscious casualties

Casualty management

A person can become unconscious following an illness or an injury. The word unconscious means that 'a person is in a state that appears like deep sleep when they lose all awareness of their surroundings'.

Casualty management is difficult, even for experienced first-aiders. Casualties have different levels of **unconsciousness**, ranging from disorientation to being completely unresponsive. The diagrams below show you the sequence of actions you must take when dealing with unconscious casualties.

To assess a casualty's level of response, we use the **A V P U** scale:

A	Alert	– The casualty is fully alert.
V	Voice	– The casualty can be confused, use inappropriate words, utter sounds or have no verbal response.
P	Pain	– The casualty may have localised pain, or can respond to pain.
U	Unresponsive	– The casualty is totally unresponsive.

Carrying out primary surveys

Checking if someone is unwell is easy if they can tell you what is wrong – but what happens if they are unconscious? The most important part of checking a casualty is to see if they are breathing, because if they are not or cannot then they may die. By using the **'head tilt, chin lift'** technique, you can assess if there is anything stopping the casualty from breathing.

The first thing you need to do is to open the airway using the **'head tilt, chin lift'** technique.

Then you can check to see if the casualty is breathing by lowering your head and **feeling on your cheek** for breath. While this is happening, look to see if the **chest is rising and falling** (a sign that the casualty is breathing).

Top Tip
Note: breathing should only be checked for a maximum of ten seconds.

Putting casualties into the recovery position

When dealing with **unconscious casualties**, the **recovery position** is a good way to ensure that a casualty's airway is kept clear and has no chance of being blocked by their tongue, by vomit or other body fluids. Putting someone in the recovery position can be done in four easy steps:

1 Place arm nearest to you at right angles to their body, elbow bent with palm up.

2 Bring the casualty's far arm across their chest and hold the back of that hand against their cheek.

3 With your other hand, grasp the leg on the far side of the casualty's knee and roll them towards you onto their side.

4 Adjust the casualty's knee (nearest to you) so that the hip and knee are at right angles.

If a casualty is unconscious

What do you do if a casualty is unconscious and is responding? (See AVPU description on page 88)

Check the area for danger → Check to see if the casualty is responding → Place in recovery position → Go and get help → Return to the casualty

What do you do if a casualty is unconscious and not responding?

Check the area for danger → Check to see if the casualty is responding → Shout for help → Check if casualty is breathing → Place in recovery position → Go and get help → Return to the casualty

✎ Quick Test

1 How can a casualty become unconscious?

2 What does AVPU stand for?

3 What position should you place an unconscious casualty in?

4 What technique would you use to check that a casualty is breathing?

Answers 1 After sustaining an injury or by having an illness. **2** Alert-Voice-Pain-Unresponsive. **3** The recovery position. **4** The 'head tilt, chin lift' technique.

Dealing with multiple casualties

What to do

Question: What happens when there is more than one casualty to treat?

Answer: You have to prioritise the treatment given to the casualties.

When there is more than one casualty to deal with, you have to adopt a method called **triage**. Triage is a method of ordering sick or injured patients according to the seriousness of their conditions. This is to ensure that medical facilities and staff are used most effectively and that the sickest and most injured casualties are dealt with first.

Top Tip
Triage may be part of the scenarios you will experience during the assessment.

How do we do this?

Here is an example of a **triage** situation:

| A casualty with a broken leg | A casualty who has cut themselves | Unconscious casualty in water |

Examine the casualties above to determine who should receive treatment first.

+ No. 1 – casualty with a broken leg. Although they will be in a lot of pain, the casualty is talking, they are awake and communicating.

+ No. 2 – casualty has a small cut on their arm. It looks like a bad injury, as there is blood coming out of the arm; however, the casualty is awake and talking.

+ No. 3 – casualty is face down in water. The casualty is not responding so we can assume they are unconscious. Because the casualty is face down in water this is a potential drowning incident.

Who would you treat first?

1st	No. 3	The casualty is unconscious and not responding to you. The casualty could have sustained other injuries which have caused them to become unconscious – for example, they may have hit the bottom of the pool with their head. They are also face down in water, which means they could drown.
2nd	No. 1	The casualty here is conscious and will be in a great deal of pain. A casualty with a broken bone will always need to go to hospital for treatment.
3rd	No. 2	Although the casualty has cut their arm, and it is a small cut, and the casualty is conscious, it will still need treatment.

First-aid kits

It is a legal requirement that all organisations (centres, schools, offices, etc) supply first-aid kits and have enough of these for their staff and clients. The type, number and contents of first-aid kits will depend on the environment people are working in.

First-aid kits should be easily accessible to everybody and their contents should be updated and checked regularly to ensure that the 'best before' dates have not expired and that there is nothing missing.

Although the contents may vary, **all first-aid kits will have the following contents**.

+ First-aid guidance leaflet and contents list
+ First-aid gloves (disposable)
+ Triangular bandages
+ Selection of plasters
+ Cleaning wipes (non-alcohol)
+ Safety pins
+ Wound dressings
+ Pencil and paper
+ Coins (for phone box)

Some other items that could be in a first-aid kit:

+ Scissors
+ Surgical tape
+ Cling film
+ Aprons

Top Tip

It is important that no medication (such as headache tablets) is included in any first-aid kit.

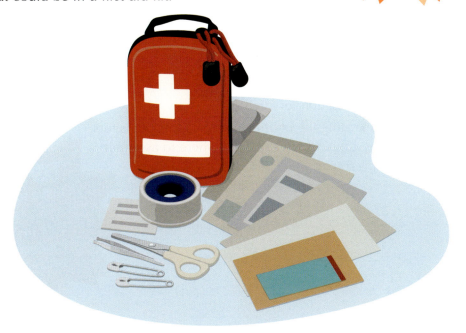

Dealing with emergencies: fire

Fire-safety policy

As mentioned on page 28, all organisations and centres have policies and procedures for all staff to comply with when incidents occur. These procedures include fires.

Centres and organisations need to train their staff and make sure that clients and visitors are familiar with what to do in the event of a fire.

Organisations are required to:

+ Keep all fire exits clear. Clear away rubbish and put away equipment. Watch out, clients could also have blocked fire exits with their bags, coats and so on.

+ Clearly display fire-exit routes. These should be clearly displayed above and beside doors (they can be illuminated or glow-in-the-dark signs). Drawings of the facility showing fire exits and routes may also be put up in public areas to assist staff and clients.

+ Carry out fire drills on a regular basis. These will allow staff to be familiar with the correct fire-drill procedures. They will also allow the centre to check if fire sensors and alarms are working.

+ Keep a record of any 'real fires' or 'simulated fires' (fire drills).

Fire safety for staff and clients includes:

+ **induction** for staff;

+ walk-around familiarisation for clients;

+ verbally communicating the information to clients or visitors about where they can find fire exits and where to assemble in case the alarms sound.

Top Tip
'REMEMBER: GET OUT – CALL THE BRIGADE OUT – STAY OUT'
(Strathclyde Fire and Rescue)

Top Tip
Make sure you know where the fire exits are in your centre or organisation.

Dealing with emergencies: unlawful entry and theft

Best practice

In case of **unlawful entry and theft** it is important that the **following actions are carried out**:

+ leave everything the way it was found, do not touch anything;
+ inform the person responsible as soon as possible;
+ make a note of your actions, including times and dates;
+ note down details of the incident as you found it, and give this to the person responsible;
+ do not allow anyone else to enter the area until you are told to;
+ follow the instructions given by the person responsible at all times.

When an **incident of theft** has taken place it is also **important do the following**:

+ make a note of what the victim says, including dates, times and the person's name and address;
+ give reassurance to the victim;
+ inform the person responsible as soon as possible;
+ pass on the information you have collected;
+ follow the instructions given by the person responsible at all times.

Top Tip
Make sure you know your centre/organisation's policies for dealing with unlawful entry and theft.

Quick Test

1 Why must you keep fire exits clear?

2 Why must all staff and clients have fire-safety awareness?

3 Who would you report to if you found signs of theft?

4 In the event of unlawful entry, why must you leave everything the way it was found?

Dealing with emergencies: missing people and suspicious strangers

Missing people

People go missing for a variety of reasons. They could be lost, children could be playing games or simply going to the toilet without informing anyone.

It is important that you **keep calm and follow procedure** in the event of someone going missing. Examples of these procedures are:

+ inform the person responsible;
+ have a good look around the organisation/centre;
+ gather information from people;
+ carry out any instructions given to you by the person responsible.

Suspicious strangers

Suspicious strangers can be anyone; they can simply be people in the wrong place at the wrong time. However, it is important that when you are dealing with incidents involving suspicious strangers you **follow procedure at all times** and:

+ inform the person responsible and explain your suspicions;
+ follow the instructions given by the person responsible.

If you are approached by someone else who is **reporting a suspicious stranger, it is important that you**:

+ note any details down that are given to you;
+ give the details to the person responsible as soon as possible;
+ follow the instructions given by the person responsible.

Top Tip
It is important that you do not deal with any incidents involving missing people or suspicious strangers yourself.

Scenarios

In this Unit, candidates are required to carry out scenarios that will reinforce their knowledge of dealing with accidents and emergencies. Scenarios will cover most aspects of knowledge and understanding in the Skills for Work Unit.

Scenarios are simulations of real events or incidents and you may be asked to take part as a casualty or as the member of staff coming to the aid of a casualty. These scenarios are designed to be realistic and should be set in a sport-and-recreation environment.

You may be working in pairs or in a small group and you will be given a briefing sheet that explains what you have to do and what part you will have to play.

It is important to remember that you are only expected to carry out the tasks set within your level of responsibility.

For example:

Who does what	What you have to do
Candidate No. 1 (is the casualty)	You were running along the edge of the swimming pool and slipped, banging the back of your head. You now have to pretend that your head really hurts.
Candidate No. 2 (is the rescuer)	You have been alerted by a member of the public that someone has fallen over and hurt their head. You will approach the person and ask questions, reassure the casualty and find the person responsible to deal with the accident.

Quick Test

1 Who must you inform if there is a report of a missing person?

2 What must you follow at all times when an incident occurs?

3 What must you do in an incident that involves a suspicious stranger?

4 What must you do if someone reports a suspicious stranger?

Answers: 1 The person responsible. **2** The organisation/centre's procedures. **3** Inform the person responsible and follow their instructions. **4** Make a note of their concerns, give the details to the person responsible and follow their instructions.

Knowledge and understanding quiz

Taking the test

To pass this Unit, all candidates will have to take a Knowledge and Understanding test to confirm that they have an adequate knowledge and understanding of accidents and emergencies.

Page reference	Question
27	What three procedures must you carry out when dealing with injuries or illnesses?
27	What three procedures must you apply when dealing with emergencies?
28	What does **NOP** stand for?
28	What does **EAP** stand for?
28	What four processes do organisations have to identify for first-aid and emergencies procedures and policies?
29	Can you name three examples of what must be contained in a **NOP**?
29	Can you name three examples of what must be contained in a **EAP**?
30	Whose safety is most important above anyone else's?
30	What four points must you think of before entering an accident or emergency situation?
31	What report must you complete when an injury or an illness has occurred?
31	What report must you complete when there has been a fire?
31	Where must all reports be stored?
32	Can you name three different types of minor injuries?
32	Who can give treatment for a minor injury?
33	Can you name three different types of major injuries?
33	Who can give treatment for a major injury?
34	Can you name three different types of minor illnesses?
34	Who can give treatment for a minor illness?
35	Can you name three different types of major illness?
35	Who can give treatment for a major illness?
36	What does **AVPU** stand for?

Page reference	Question
36	What technique should you use to assess if there is anything stopping a casualty from breathing?
36	What two signs do you look for when checking to see if a casualty is breathing?
37	What position should you place a casualty in if they are unconscious?
38	What is the term used when dealing with more than one casualty?
39	Name four items that should be contained in a first-aid kit.
39	Can you name two other items that **COULD** be contained in a first-aid kit?
40	Name three things organisations are required to do to ensure the safety of people in the event of a fire.
40	Name two ways that staff and clients can get to know what to do in the event of a fire.
41	Name three actions you need to carry out when dealing with unlawful entry and theft.
41	Name two actions you have to do when theft has taken place.
42	What must you do if someone goes missing?
42	Name two examples of a missing-persons procedure.
42	What must you follow if there has been a report of a suspicious stranger?
42	What three procedures must you follow when a report of a suspicious stranger has been made to you?

Answers: 27 Assess the area, get help, wear personal protective equipment (PPE) 27 Assess the area, get help, do not deal with anything 28 Normal Operating Plan 28 Emergency Action Plan 28 Hazards, consequences, likelihood, reduce the risk 29 Choose any four of the ten bullet points 29 Choose any three out of the four bullet points 30 Yourself 30 Find out about the incident and inform the person responsible, assess the scene, report back only to the person responsible, wear correct PPE 31 Accident report 31 Emergency report 31 In a safe location 32 Choose three out of the five in the table 32 By a first-aider (the person responsible) 33 Choose any three out of the six in the table 33 Medical assistance e.g. paramedics, doctors 34 Choose any three out of the ten in the table 34 First-aider (person responsible) 35 Choose any three out of the twelve 35 Medical assistance 36 Alert, Voice, Pain, Unresponsive 36 Head tilt/chin lift 36 Breathing on your cheek, chest rising and falling 37 The recovery position 38 Triage 39 Choose any four out of the first bulleted list 39 Choose any two out of the second bulleted list 40 Choose any three out of the first bulleted list 40 Choose any two out of the second bulleted list 41 Choose any three out of the first bulleted list 41 Choose any two out of the second bulleted list 42 Keep calm and follow the organisation/centre procedures 42 Choose any two out of the first bulleted list 42 Follow the organisation/centre procedures at all times 42 Note any details given to you, give the details to the person responsible and follow their instructions

Dealing with facilities and equipment

Best practice

This Unit is designed to enable you to gain practical experience in setting up, taking down and storing a variety of equipment, as well as ensuring that facilities are kept clean and tidy. It is important that you do these tasks with the person responsible present at all times.

When dealing with any kind of equipment, it is important that all aspects of health and safety procedure are followed – for example, moving and handling large pieces of equipment, using appropriate **personal protective equipment (PPE)** and following all the centre's procedures for setting up, taking down and storing equipment, and the cleaning and tidying of facility areas.

When you are dealing with equipment, you will learn how to:

- locate the correct equipment for the activity;
- check the equipment for faults, damage or missing parts;
- ensure the equipment is set up on time for the activity;
- ensure the the equipment is set up safely according to manufacturers' guidelines;
- make reports on unserviceable equipment.

When taking down equipment you will learn to:

- check the equipment after use for faults, damage or missing parts;
- ensure that the equipment is handled in a way that does not damage either you or the equipment;
- store it in its correct location, so that it is ready to use again;
- ensure that storage areas are kept clean and tidy;
- remove faulty or damaged equipment.

Cleaning and tidying

Lastly, in this Unit you will be introduced to how organisations and centres are correctly cleaned and tidied. With the person responsible, you will agree a schedule for these duties to be carried out. You will also learn how to:

- clean and tidy areas using the correct PPE and materials;
- follow the organisation's procedures for carrying out any scheduled cleaning and tidying duties;
- identify the appropriate materials for the job;
- correctly dispose of spillages, breakages and waste;
- ensure that materials are correctly stored in line with organisational and health-and-safety procedures;
- maintain areas within a centre or organisation to ensure that all emergency exits are kept clear.

In this Unit you will learn the basics of health and safety as it is relevant to the setting up and taking down of equipment, and you will gain a basic overview of COSHH (Control of Substances Hazardous to Health), basic manual handling techniques and the correct PPE (Personal Protective Equipment) and equipment for the duties you will be carrying out.

What employability skills are in this Unit?

You will have the opportunity to develop a range of employability skills, including:

 taking advice/taking advice from others;

 wearing appropriate dress;

 awareness of health and safety procedures;

 following instructions.

Top Tip
Look out for the symbol to see where the employability skills have been covered

Top Tip
Remember, any words in GREEN are explained in the GLOSSARY section on pages 92 and 93.

Planning schedules

The scheduled log

In this Unit, you will have to assist the person responsible in carrying out a range of tasks that involve equipment and the facilities.

With the person responsible, you will agree a list of tasks (or jobs) that need to be carried out over a set period of time. These tasks need to be recorded on a log along with timings of when the tasks have to be done.

Top Tip
Work with the person responsible and find out what your tasks are.

This scheduled log contains:

- what the task is – for example, setting up equipment for an activity;
- the time when the tasks have to be carried out by, and how long you have to complete them;
- sections for you and the person responsible to sign when the work has been carried out.

Log 1			
Time	**Task**	**Candidate signature**	**Person responsible signature**
9:00am	Clean and tidy changing-room areas, before 9:30am		
10:00am	Set up kayaks and paddles for group of eight, before 10:30am		
2:00pm	Take down badminton equipment, by 2:30pm		
2:30pm	Tidy entrance area and empty bins		

There may be occasions when additional tasks will have to be completed over and above the daily schedule for that day.

Log 2		
Task	**Candidate signature**	**Person responsible signature**
Empty bins and dispose of rubbish around the centre		
Tidy entrance hall and replace any promotional material		

Being in the right place at the right time

When undertaking tasks in the centre or organisation, it is important to use your time efficiently and plan when tasks need to be completed. You need to **manage your time**. You may have to juggle tasks around in order to become efficient and ensure that the tasks are completed on time.

For example: You have planned your schedule for the day and agreed which tasks you will be assisting the person responsible with (see Logs 1 and 2 on previous page).

Table 1 shows you that these two tasks have to be carried out at specific times. What this means is that these tasks must be completed by a certain time. Reasons could be:

- the centre has to be clean and tidy for clients before it opens;
- activities are due to begin at a certain time;
- another activity is using the same facility (such as a sports hall) and may have to be set up straight afterwards.

Managing your time around these set tasks will allow you to fit in other routine tasks (see **Log 2** on previous page). From **Log 1**, you can see that there are three-and-a-half hours between one set task and another, which means that this would be the ideal time to carry out the daily routine tasks.

Top Tip
Find out how your daily routine tasks can be fitted into your scheduled log.

Health and safety: dealing with equipment

General guidelines

By law, all organisations and activity centres produce **guidelines** for their staff on how to conduct themselves when dealing with equipment. Organisations do this in order to protect anyone who uses the equipment (staff and clients).

Before anyone is allowed to deal with any piece of equipment, all members of staff take part in an induction where they are shown how to correctly set up and take down the equipment. During this induction, they may be shown how to look for faults or damage which would make the equipment unserviceable and potentially dangerous.

The guidelines are also in place to ensure the safety of clients using the centre's equipment because the centre has a **duty of care** towards the people who use their facilities. Failure to keep clients safe from harm could be judged to be negligent.

When you are dealing with equipment you will be working with the **person responsible**.

Examples of the kind of health and safety training you will receive when dealing with equipment are:

- knowing how to set up and take down equipment according to organisational procedures;
- checking equipment for damage, faults and missing parts;
- correct handling of equipment;
- dealing with damaged equipment and completing the correct reports.

Top Tip

Find out from the person responsible what the guidelines are in your centre for dealing with equipment.

Introduction to manual handling

The *Manual Handling Operations Regulations* 1992 (amended in 2002) cover a wide range of activities that involve lifting, carrying, pushing, pulling or lowering. This means that there are regulations that employers, trainers and so on have to comply with in order to ensure the safety of staff, students or clients.

For example:

Cricket:	the equipment you have to set up is: stumps, bats and leg padding.	The equipment is light and easy for one person to set up.
Canoeing:	The equipment you have to remove from storage is: four canoes.	The canoes are heavy, therefore two people are needed to carry them.

If you have to move, lift or pull any type of equipment, it is important you follow the simple steps below:

Look at the task Does it involve lifting heavy equipment or carrying equipment over long distances? Consider getting help or using trolleys or other devices designed to do the job.

What will you be carrying? Is the equipment heavy, difficult to grasp or loaded awkwardly? Consider reducing the amount you carry or use other devices that are designed to do the job.

Where are you going? Where are you transporting the equipment? Is the floor/ground slippery or uneven, or will there be difficult weather conditions? Consider wearing appropriate PPE, and perhaps alternative venues. If alternative venues cannot be found, help and assistance will need to be found.

Top Tip
What types of equipment will you be handling? Do you need one person to set up and take down the equipment, or many people?

 Quick Test

1 What must staff follow to ensure the safety of other members of staff and clients?

2 Who will you be working with when setting up and taking down equipment?

3 What regulations must you follow when handling large or heavy pieces of equipment?

4 How many people are needed to set up small and easy pieces of equipment?

Answers: 1 Centre guidelines. **2** The person responsible. **3** Manual Handling Operations Regulations. **4** One.

Identifying equipment and checking for faults

Identifying equipment

On your course you will learn how to identify the correct equipment for specific sports. You will be shown which pieces of equipment are used for a range of different sports when **setting up and taking down** equipment.

Checking for faults

Do not assume that all the equipment stored away is ready to use, or that when an activity has finished the equipment can be put away immediately after use. It is important that all equipment is checked for:

- **faults**: for example, deflated footballs;
- **damage**: for example, chipped/dented floats for swimming;
- **missing parts**: for example, drainage bungs on kayaks.

As all staff within centres are trained to deal with equipment within their level of responsibility, it is essential that these checks are carried out **according to the centre/organisation and manufacturer's guidelines**. It is also a health and safety requirement that equipment is set up and taken down safely, and that it does not cause any harm to staff or clients.

Top Tip
If equipment is found to have a fault, be damaged or have missing parts, make sure the relevant report is filled out.

First steps

When you are assisting the person responsible setting up and taking down equipment, it is important that all health and safety rules are followed at all times.

Do I need help? Bear in mind that larger or heavier pieces of equipment may need more than one person to move into position. Some larger or heavier equipment may have its own specialist piece of machinery to move it into position, for example, a trolley. If you have any doubts, ask the person responsible.

Setting up equipment

When setting up equipment, it is important that:

- it is set up in **the correct location**. For example, some centres use sports halls for different types of activities, and as a result the floor will be marked for multiple activities – for example, basketball, tennis, football and so on. If you are setting up for a badminton session, make sure that the net is set on the lines marked for badminton!

- it is set up at **the correct time**. Equipment is usually set up *BEFORE* an activity session begins. Therefore it is important that, if the task is to set up equipment for an *activity that begins* at 10:30am, the equipment must be set up before this time in order for *the activity to start on time*.

Taking down equipment

Points to consider when taking down equipment.

- **Be on time**. If your schedule states that you should take down equipment at a specific time, this is usually because there could be a different activity using the sports hall immediately afterwards.

- **Stick to the manufacturer's and centre guidelines**. Make sure that you take down equipment safely. This is for your safety and for that of others.

Top Tip
To find out when equipment has to be set up and taken down look at your Schedule Log.

Quick Test

1 What must you check before any equipment is set up and when it is taken down?

2 How should equipment be set up and taken down?

3 What two important points must you make sure are done when setting up equipment?

4 What two important points must you make sure are done when taking down equipment?

Answers: 1 For faults, damage and missing parts. **2** According to the centre, organisation and manufacturer's requirements. **3** In the right location at the right time. **4** Be on time and adhere to the manufacturer's and centre guidelines.

Safe storage

For health and safety reasons, it is important that all storage areas are kept in a clean and tidy condition. Also consider how you put away equipment in a store to ensure that accessibility and safety are maintained at all times.

Good examples

A good example of a store.

- Clearly labelled areas for sports equipment – this helps with storing equipment in specific places for specific sports.

- Separate areas for every type of sporting equipment – this way, it is easy to find sports equipment for the next session without spending time trying to find all the necessary pieces.

- Large or heavy equipment on floor level – the equipment is easier to retrieve and it is safer than placing it up high where it may do harm by falling.

- Small items bagged or boxed up – this keeps storage areas clear of equipment and makes them easier to retrieve. Keeping small items bagged or boxed prevents people from falling over them.

- Access kept clear – this enables people to get in and out of the storage area, but it will also enable you to remove or store equipment more easily and will ensure the safety of anyone who enters the store.

- Clean equipment – this is always good practice. When setting up and storing equipment, always clean the equipment ready for the next session. By cleaning equipment, you may find any breakages or faults that you have missed before!

Bad examples

The list above shows you what a good store looks like. A **bad store** has:

- dirty equipment;
- items of equipment stored randomly;
- restricted access;
- large or heavy items unsecured and stored high;
- equipment stored wherever there is space!

Top Tip
Ask the person responsible how different items of equipment should be stored in your facility.

Equipment – reporting of faults, damage and missing parts

Set procedures

In centres there are **set procedures** that staff have to follow when dealing with problems they may have with pieces of equipment. It is important that you report anything you find wrong with a piece of equipment and that you follow the centre's procedures also. There are different ways to report problems.

- **Verbally**: to the person responsible or manager.
- **Written**: in the centre's equipment log.

Date	Time	Details of Report
1/6/07	9.30am	Large sections of the swimming floats were missing – need replacement floats
5/6/07	2.30pm	Five footballs have punctures – need repairs or need replacement balls
27/6/07	12.30pm	Clips on rucksacks are missing – need replacments

Usually if you have to report that a piece of equipment is damaged, faulty or has missing parts, the items are removed **immediately** from the store and placed into a **separate area** designated specially for this use. If the centre does not have a separate area, they mark the equipment in some way to highlight to others that a particular piece of equipment is not to be used.

By removing these damaged items from the normal store, you are ensuring that they will not be used until they are fixed or replaced.

Top Tip
Ask the person responsible where the equipment goes if it is faulty, damaged or has missing parts.

Quick Test

1 Why must you store equipment safely?

2 When storing equipment, what must you ensure at all times?

3 What must you follow when reporting problems with equipment?

4 What two different ways can you make a report?

Answers: 1 For health and safety reasons. **2** Accessibility and safety are maintained. **3** Set procedures. **4** Verbally and written.

Cleaning facility areas

Introduction

This section of the Unit introduces you to how facilities are cleaned and tidied. You will assist the person responsible while they carry out cleaning and tidying tasks around a centre. These tasks will be agreed beforehand and written down in a **log**.

It is very important that, while you are carrying out cleaning tasks, you follow the **COSHH** regulations and policies/procedures laid down by the centre at all times. These policies and procedures relate to:

- how you should use cleaning materials – which chemicals can you mix, is there a certain way you should use them, such as dilute with water?
- which cleaning materials you use and where you can use them – some cleaning materials may be corrosive or abrasive to certain surfaces and can only be used for a specific purpose;
- what personal protective equipment you should wear – each cleaning and tidying duty may require you to wear a specific type of PPE;
- how cleaning materials should be stored – where you can store them and how they are stored. This could mean that some chemicals cannot be stored next to each other.

Cleaning – personal protective equipment (PPE)

It is the centre's duty to provide staff with the relevant PPE and to ensure that staff are trained and wear their PPE. PPE relates to equipment you should wear while carrying out any cleaning tasks. Some examples are:

- aprons,
- gloves,
- masks,
- boots.

Top Tip
Make sure you wear the correct PPE when carrying out cleaning tasks.

Top Tip
Find out which items of PPE you need to wear when carrying out cleaning tasks at your facility.

COSHH

In a working environment where any type of hazardous substance is used or is present – for example, swimming-pool chemicals, washing-up liquid, floor cleaner, toilet cleaner, and so on. It is the law that all organisations and centres have to comply with a set of regulations called **COSHH**, which means:

Control

Of

Substances

Hazardous to

Health

These regulations are designed to protect employers, staff, clients and anyone else who may be exposed to **hazardous substances**. A hazardous substance can make someone ill, if the person has:

- **Ingested** – by swallowing

- **Inhaled** – breathing in fumes (smoke, airborne particles)

- **Absorbed** – through the skin (this may be a liquid, powder, cream or gel-like substance)

- **Injected** – through the skin straight into the body via sharp objects such as a needle.

COSHH regulations ensure that centres and organisations do the following:

- assess the hazard, minimise the risk and put control measures in place;
- make sure staff are trained to handle hazardous substances;
- have plans and procedures in place to deal with accidents and emergencies.

Quick Test

1 What regulations do you need to follow when carrying out cleaning tasks?

2 What does PPE stand for?

3 What must you ensure when carrying out cleaning and tidying duties?

4 Who will you be working with when carrying out any cleaning and tidying tasks?

Answers: 1 COSHH. **2** Personal Protective Equipment **3** You cause as little disruption as possible. **4** The person responsible.

Keeping areas clean and tidy

Rotas and tasks

In most centres and organisations, staff have rotas for when they are to carry out cleaning and tidying tasks. These are usually scheduled **to cause as little disruption as possible** to other members of staff and clients using the centre. Staff may have one or more kinds of schedules. The first may be one that directly relates to the activities taking place or the client groups who are in for that day. Another might detail the daily duties that need to be carried out such as general cleaning, tidying and maintaining of facility areas.

You will be carrying out scheduled cleaning and tidying tasks while you complete this aspect of the Unit. Your general daily duties may require you to tidy facility areas. You may be asked to:

- empty bins,
- check for litter,
- tidy up notice boards and put up new promotional material.

You may also need to ensure that fire exits and fire-exit routes:

- are clear of any waste materials, inside and outside,
- have fire action notices are in place (including evacuation routes),
- are clear of any obstructions.

Duties specific to that day will depend on the centre you are in. These duties could be:

- cleaning a particular room ready for an activity,
- checking that there is no rubbish in activity sites,
- ensuring that all safety equipment is where it should be.

Dealing with spillages and breakages

All centres will have a procedure on how to deal with spillages and breakages. When you are informed that a spillage or a breakage has taken place, make sure you **inform the person responsible** and assist them in dealing with the incident. Make sure that you have the correct PPE and cleaning materials.

It is important you make sure that you **follow the centre's guidelines** at all times and that the appropriate signage is put up informing people of the hazard so that it does not cause an accident, such as people slipping or cutting themselves.

The types of **spillages** you may encounter are:

- from drinks,
- from body fluids (blood, urine, etc),
- spillages found in sports areas, such as water on a swimming-pool side, or leaks from windows.

Types of **breakages** you may encounter from broken equipment:

- sports equipment – goal nets,
- safety equipment – throw lines (pool).

Types of breakages within the facility may include:

- window glass,
- bottles,
- chairs.

T☀p Tip
Ask the person responsible how you are to deal with any spillage and breakages.

Quick Test

1 What does COSHH stand for?

2 What four ways can a hazardous substance make someone ill?

3 Who must you inform if a spillage or a breakage has occurred?

4 What must you follow when a spillage or a breakage has occurred?

Answers: 1 Control Of Substances Hazardous to Health. **2** Ingested, inhaled, absorbed, injected. **3** The person responsible. **4** The centre guidelines.

Maintenance

Dealing with incidents

To maintain areas in a safe and tidy condition, you have to ensure that incidents are **dealt with quickly and efficiently**, without disturbing staff and clients who are using the facility, whilst keeping them safe from harm.

Spillages, breakages or waste must be dealt with according to the centre's procedures by using the correct equipment and PPE for the task. The person responsible will be able to help you with these tasks and provide training and guidance on how to deal with these types of incidents.

In order to keep people safe, you may be asked to use a variety of methods. These could be:

- signage – posters (area out of use/bounds),
- warning tape – used to mark off dangerous areas,
- floor signs – 'Slippery floor' signs.

Waste disposal

Another way of keeping a facility safe and ensuring the safety of the people who use it, is to dispose of waste correctly.

Waste disposal can mean many things. Most centres have specific places where waste can be disposed of, such as recycling for paper, plastic, cans and so on. However, when the waste comes from body fluids or first-aid dressings, it has to be **disposed of correctly**, especially if it involves the waste disposal of body fluids. This is to avoid cross-contamination. Centres have guidelines for dealing with different types of waste disposal. For example, waste from first-aid dressings must be disposed in the **yellow clinical waste bag or bin**.

Top Tip
Find out how your centre deals with waste disposal for different spillages and breakages.

Correct storage of cleaning and tidying materials

As mentioned on page 54, store rooms for cleaning and tidying materials should be kept **safe, clean and tidy**. The person responsible will be able to show you where cleaning materials should be kept and how to store them safely.

There are guidelines set by the manufacturers on how you must store their cleaning products. It is very important that certain cleaning chemicals are stored **according to the procedures laid down by the centre and by the manufacturer of the chemical**. This is because some chemicals react to each other, which can cause big problems – for example, giving off toxic vapours.

Unlike activity equipment, cleaning and tidying materials cannot all be kept in the same store. Some centres store cleaning materials in different places to avoid contamination. Centres and organisations sometimes colour-code their cleaning materials – for example, anything that is coloured blue = kitchen, yellow = changing rooms, red = first-aid, and so on.

Top Tip
Make sure you follow the facility's guidelines for the storage of cleaning and tidying materials.

Quick Test

1 When an incident has occurred, how should it be dealt with?

2 When dealing with waste disposal, what must you ensure?

3 How should store rooms for cleaning and tidying materials be kept?

4 How should cleaning chemicals be stored?

Answers: 1 Quickly and efficiently. **2** That it is disposed of correctly. **3** Safe, clean and tidy. **4** According to the procedures laid down by the centre and by the manufacturer of the chemical.

Assisting activity sessions

Information and planning

This Unit is designed to enable you to assist the person responsible in planning and delivering activity sessions. The person responsible will give you help and guidance on all aspects of this Unit. While you are undertaking the tasks in this Unit you will be under the direct supervision of the person responsible at all times.

You will learn how to gather information about the activity before you put together session plans. Before you can complete the activity session plans, you will be expected to gather relevant information about:

- the type of activity and what you will be assisting with;
- what kind of people will be taking part in the activity;
- what kind of activity equipment will be used and perhaps set up before the activity session begins;
- whether the activity will need any safety equipment;
- where the activity will take place and whether there is an alternative venue if the original one is not suitable;
- what kind of health and safety issues need to be addressed.

For the completion of this Unit, you will need to compile a risk assessment. Your tutor will teach you what a risk assessment is and how they are used by individuals, coaches and organisations.

Using all this information will allow you to contribute to the plan of the activity session, which will then be approved by the person responsible before the activity session begins.

What employability skills are in this section?

As you will be assisting with the activity session, you have to arrive on time, in the right place and wear appropriate clothing for the session.

You will be assisting the person responsible to give explanations and demonstrations to participants and to respond to their questions. You will need to watch participants and then give them feedback. If you encounter any problems, it is important that you refer them to the person responsible for the activity.

At the end of the activity session, you will review the activity with the participants and with the person responsible, and then compare these reviews with how well you thought the session went.

Finally, you will have a personal review with the person responsible on your performance. Aspects of the session that went well and aspects of the planning, delivery and reviewing of the activity that could be improved will be discussed.

Over this Unit, you will have the opportunity to develop the following employability skills.

 Reviewing progress/reviewing

 Dealing with customers/customer care

 Taking advice/taking advice from others

 Setting targets

 Wearing appropriate dress

 Planning and preparation

 Timekeeping

 Giving advice

 Completing tasks

Top Tip

Look out for the symbol to see where the Employability Skills have been covered.

Top Tip

Remember, any words in GREEN are explained in the GLOSSARY section on pages 93 and 94.

Gathering relevant information

Activity sessions

With the person responsible, agree what your role will be during the activity session. You will be planning activities for both an individual and a group. It is important to gather information relevant to the activity, as this information will give you an insight into all the little things you need to consider before you meet the participants.

The information you need to collect will include:

- Details about the activity – when the activity session will take place, and how long it will last.

- Why are you doing the activity? – what are the aims of the activity? Is it for fun, developing the participants' personal skills or developing teamwork within the group?

- Location of the activity – is the venue available or will another venue need to be found, is the venue for the activity suitable?

- How many participants will there be? – you will need to know how many people there will be in the group, as this could cause problems for resources (how much activity equipment is available?).

- What part of the activity session will you be planning for? – you need to know this information to help you and the person responsible plan for the session.

- The kinds of equipment you will need – **for the activity, for the participants, for yourself and for safety purposes**.

- Planning for changes to the original plan – do you have an alternative plan if, for example, the weather is very poor on the day you plan to assist with rugby training on an outside pitch?

- Planning for emergencies and incidents – 'plan B' options that can incorporate alternatives in case of an emergency. For example, if you were assisting an instructor taking a group hillwalking and an accident occured you would need to change your route to accommodate this.

Top Tip
The person responsible will be able to supply you with the information about the group that you need to complete your activity session plan.

Information on participants and dealing with confidentiality

When planning for any activity, it is important to know about the participants. You will need to know their:

- **age range,**
- **ability,**
- **medical issues.**

When acquiring this kind of information, you will have to safeguard these personal details and ensure that only the relevant people have access to it – usually only the person responsible for the activity session.

All coaches, instructors, tutors and so on, need to collect this personal information about participants before the activity session starts, as this information will enable the person responsible to make adjustments to the planned activity in plenty of time.

The person responsible may wish to change the planned activity once they have the participant information, as there could be a member of the group who requires special assistance. For example, if the activity session plan was for a hillwalk, and the personal participant information then revealed that one member of the group used a wheelchair and was unable to walk up hills or long distances, then the plan would need to be changed to accommodate this person's needs, and an alternative route would need to be found to suit all group members.

Any member of staff who directly handles personal information about others must follow the **Data Protection Act**.

Top Tip
Ensure that any information collected about participants is kept **confidential**.

Quick Test

1 What kinds of activities will you be planning a session for?

2 Name two examples of the kinds of equipment you will need for an activity.

3 When you plan for an activity, what three things do you need to know about the participants?

4 If any member of staff directly handles any personal information about others, what must they follow?

Answers: 1 For an individual and a group. **2** For any two of the following: the activity, participant, yourself, safety. **3** Age range, ability, medical issues. **4** The Data Protection Act.

Equipment

Types of equipment

When looking at what **equipment** needs to be assembled before a session starts, the types of equipment will vary depending on what the activity is and where the activity is taking place.

Equipment is split up into four main categories.

Activity equipment

Equipment you will use while you are out on activity sessions. This equipment could be: balls, tennis rackets, kayaks or floor mats.

Participant equipment

Equipment the participants need to wear. This could be: shorts, t-shirts, trainers, swimming costumes, wetsuits or tracksuits.

Own equipment

Equipment that you need to wear and use, making sure you are ready before the session begins. This equipment may be the same as the participants', with additional items such as a whistle.

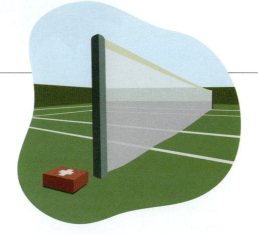

Safety equipment

This equipment is very important when you are on activities. Bring this equipment with you in case an incident occurs, for example: a first-aid kit, throw line, hot drink or warm clothes.

It is important to set up the equipment before an activity session starts. This will allow you to be ready for the activity session and will enable the activity to start on time without participants waiting around and **losing valuable activity** time.

Top Tip
Find out what equipment you need for your activity sessions.

Identifying different types of equipment

With the **person responsible**, you will have to identify the different types of equipment that are required for the activity you will be assisting. For example, what equipment would you need for a football session or a kayak session?

Activity equipment	Football pitch, goals and nets, cones, balls, bibs
Participant equipment	T-shirt, shorts, tracksuit, football boots
Own equipment	T-shirt, shorts, tracksuit, football boots, whistle
Safety equipment	First-aid kit

As you can see, setting up for a football session is quite simple. Here is an example of the equipment that might be used for a beginners' kayaking session.

Activity equipment	Kayaks, paddles, ball (for games)
Participant equipment	Swimsuits, wetsuits, cagoule, buoyancy aid, helmet, appropriate footwear (e.g. trainers)
Own equipment	Swimsuits, wetsuits, cagoule, buoyancy aid, helmet, appropriate footwear (e.g. trainers)
Safety equipment	First-aid kit, tow line, throw line

What this demonstrates is that each activity has its own list of equipment that needs to be set up before the session begins. As the activity session plan is being completed, you will need to work with the person responsible to find out what equipment is required for the activity you will be assisting.

Top Tip
Work with the person responsible to find out what equipment is needed for the activity session.

Quick Test

1 What will need to be assembled before an activity starts?

2 If equipment is not set up on time, what will happen?

3 Who will help you identify the different pieces of equipment needed for the activity?

4 Do all activities use the same equipment?

Answers: 1 The equipment. **2** You will lose valuable activity time. **3** The person responsible. **4** No.

Risk assessments

The importance of risk assessments

Risk assessments are an important process where you identify potential hazards and look to see how these can be made safe by highlighting the relevant practical steps that need to be taken to reduce the risk for you and your group. Every centre or organisation has a risk assessment for every activity that they offer to participants. Risk assessments not only cover activities, but also cover other potential hazards in the centre/organisation, inside and outside.

Before you plan your activity session, it is important that you and the person responsible carry out a risk assessment. By following the steps below, you can easily put together a risk assessment for your activity.

Identifying the hazards

Have a look at the drawing below. The hazard in this picture is the **water on the floor**.

Who will the hazard affect?

Have another look at the drawing. You can see that **everyone** will be affected.

How will the hazard affect everyone?

The hazard effect here has been that the individual has **slipped** and fallen.

Top Tip
When writing up a risk assessment, only note down hazards that will affect the activity you are assisting with.

Putting in control measures

Now you can see that the control measure in this situation would be to inform everybody that there is a hazard up ahead by putting up a **sign**. Now when anyone approaches the water, they will know that it's there and will walk round it safely (see picture below).

Ratings

Ratings are given to show the seriousness of a hazard. These ratings are on a scale of **1 (low)**, **2 (medium)**, **3 (high)**:

	Risk rating
1 What would be the risk rating for someone who has slipped and fallen?	2
2 What would be the likelihood of it actually happening?	× 2
Multiplying these two figures together will give you a risk rating before you put in control measures (the 'slippery floor' sign)	= 4
3 What would happen to this rating when you DO put the control measures in place? It will reduce it to:	1
What would the NEW risk rating for the wet floor be, now you have the 'slippery floor' sign in place? (To find this out, you need to multiply points 2 and 3.) As you can see, the risk has been significantly reduced by identifying the hazard and putting up a sign.	= 2

Top Tip
Risk ratings are a way of seeing how serious a hazard is. When you have put in your control measures, this rating will fall, therefore significantly reducing the risk to everyone.

Quick Test

1 What process identifys potential hazards?

2 Who can be affected by a hazard?

3 What was the control measure put in place to warn people of the hazard?

4 What is the risk rating scale?

Answers: 1 Risk assessments. **2** Everyone. **3** A sign. **4** 1 (low), 2 (medium), 3 (high).

Creating an activity session plan

Activity session plans

Every coach, tutor or instructor who has taken an activity session has, at some point, completed a session plan for a group or for an individual. Plans give the session some structure (showing a breakdown of what is contained in the activity session, which includes timings), and allows you to cover all the main aims and objectives of the activity in the time available.

You will be assisting the person responsible with an activity session plan based on an agreed activity. It is essential that all activity session plans are completed **before** the activity begins, as this will allow any alterations to be made and will allow you and the person responsible to decide whether the content of the activity session plan is:

- correct and you are able to carry out those activities;
- allows for changes to be made to the activity session plan;
- ensures that the plan is ready before the activity goes ahead.

Once the plan has been approved, the **person responsible** will then sign and date it to indicate that the activity session is now ready to go ahead.

T⚙p Tip
A coach, instructor, tutor, or teacher can sign off your activity session plan, but essentially they will be the *person responsible* for taking the activity session.

The contents of a plan

For your **assessment** you will be asked to complete an activity session plan which your tutor/assessor will give to you. Activity session plans may contain the following:

What the activity is and where it is taking place	Activity: *Nature walk* Venue: *Forest track, Loch Lomond*
Day, time, and how long it will last for – e.g. three hours	Date: *14/07/07* Time: From: *9.30am* To: *12.30 pm*
Information about the group or individual – e.g. health issues	Info on group: *two participants have Asthma*
What equipment you will be using – e.g. equipment for yourself, for the activity, for safety and for the participants	Own equipment: *rucksack, boots, waterproofs* Activity equipment: *group shelter, radio* Safety equipment: *first-aid kit* Participant equipment: *boots, waterproofs*
If equipment needs to be set up before the session begins – note down the equipment, for example, goals for football	Equipment that needs to be set up: *Ensure that relevant safety equipment and group shelters are available for the day*
Noting down any predictable changes of circumstances – e.g. weather	Predictable changes of circumstances: *Weather conditions changing and participant emergencies*
Main aim of the session – e.g. individual skills, teamwork.	Aim of session: *give participants an experience of nature that uses their senses*
Your involvement in the activity – e.g. your role during the activity	My involvement: *to assist the person responsible with two activities*
What are the main teaching points – e.g. how to use a kayak paddle when kayaking forward	Teaching points: *assist participants with an activity:* *1) that used their smelling sense,* *2) that used their listening sense.*

Top Tip

The person responsible will be able to supply the relevant information necessary to complete all sections of the activity session plan.

Quick Test

1 When should activity session plans be completed?

2 Who will sign and date the activity session plan once it has been approved?

3 When will you need to complete your activity session plans for?

4 Give an example of the kind of information you will need to complete in the section for information on the group.

Answers: 1 Before the session begins. **2** The person responsible. **3** Before assessment. **4** Health issues, age, ability.

Assisting with activity sessions

Arriving on time

Activity sessions are usually booked in advance and there can be more than one activity using the facilities and the equipment on that day. It is important that you arrive **on time** to start your activity session – even better, be ten minutes early. This way, you can meet the group arriving and start on time.

Being on time is a skill most people have, and it is a good skill to show employers, teachers and instructors that you are keen to do the activity. It also reflects positively on your school, college or centre.

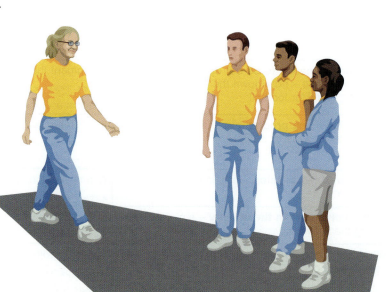

Wearing the correct clothes

When turning up to assist with activity sessions, it is important to dress appropriately for the session. Centres usually give their **staff uniforms** and expect them to wear these, as part of **health and safety** requirements and to promote their corporate image. They will also have adopted a policy on jewellery. In most cases, all jewellery has to be removed, or you must tape over items that cannot be removed. Again, this is for **health and safety** reasons – imagine assisting with an activity and accidentally your earring gets ripped out!

You may need to ensure that participants remove jewellery and are dressed appropriately, especially if the activity is taking part outside. For example, for football training outside in winter, you would expect the participants to be wearing warm clothing (tracksuits, jumpers or jackets).

Top Tip
Did you know it is negligent to take participants out on activities without the correct clothing?

Explanations and demonstrations

How you **explain the activity** or tasks to a group will mean the difference between the participants carrying out the tasks you set them, or not. Consider the following when explaining an activity or task to a group:

- talk slowly and clearly;
- face in the direction of the group;
- be prepared to repeat your explanation!

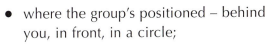

Demonstrations can show participants clearly what you want them to do. Not all participants may understand what you are saying, especially if they are new to the sport. Consider the following when carrying out demonstrations:

- where the group's positioned – behind you, in front, in a circle;
- position yourself so that you can see all the participants – if you can see them, they can see you!
- if demonstrating outside, consider the weather conditions and where it would be best to demonstrate – a sheltered area, away from the sun and so on;
- slow your demonstration down;
- repeat your demonstration.

T☀p Tip
Have you tried explaining an activity without talking?

Quick Test

1 When must you arrive for the activity?

2 What might centres give their staff to dress in?

3 Why must you follow the centre's policy for the wearing of jewellery?

4 What two techniques do you carry out to show participants how to do an activity?

Answers: 1 On time. **2** Staff uniforms. **3** For health and safety. **4** Explain the activity and demonstrate.

73

Providing feedback

Why do we do it?

When assisting the person responsible with an activity session, there will come a time when you will have to provide feedback to participants on their performance. This feedback has to be **constructive** in order to give the participant encouragement as well as correcting faults.

It is important that the feedback you give is **constructive** so that participants remain enthusiastic and are not put off by negative comments.

How is it done?

A slice of cake, for example, can be split up into three sections:

Top section

In the top section, you will be giving PRAISE, for example:

'**well done**' or '**that was a good try**'.

Middle section

In the middle section, you will be giving feedback on performance, pointing out aspects of performance that may need to be improved, for example, '**you need to turn with the ball quicker**'.

Bottom section

In the bottom section, you will be giving **encouragement**, allowing participants to continue with the activity, for example: '**let's see you give it a try**'.

Dealing with problems and questions

Participants will always have problems and questions about anything that is explained or demonstrated in an activity session. How you go about addressing these is crucial to the group's enjoyment and learning experience, and dealing with these issues is an important aspect of customer care.

If you have to deal with a problem, it is usually best to find out exactly **what the problem is** and then refer it to the person responsible for the activity.

Problems can come from a variety of sources. Some examples are:

- injuries or other types of emergencies – someone has been hurt and needs first aid, or someone has gone missing from a group;
- problems with being unable to perform a task – the task may be too difficult, or they may not have understood the explanations that you or the person responsible gave;
- problems with other members of the group – this can arise if the group members do not know one another and are taking part in team games – or there could be personality clashes within the team.

Questions that you may encounter can come from anywhere. Again, **customer care** is important, some examples of the types of questions you may be able to answer:

- what a particular piece of equipment is called;
- where the toilets are and whether the participant can go;
- how to do something;
- where they can get information about other activity sessions.

What's that?

Can you show me how to do that again?

T✹p Tip
If in doubt, refer any questions to the person responsible!

✎ Quick Test

1 How must feedback be delivered to participants?

2 What three sections does feedback get split up into?

3 When dealing with problems, what is it best to find out?

4 Problems are linked to what other type of care?

Answers: 1 Feedback has to be constructive. **2** Top, middle and bottom sections; praise, advice and encouragement. **3** What the problems are. **4** Customer care.

Reviewing

Reviewing with participants

Usually, the content of what you review with participants will be linked to their aims for the activity session, for example:

- fun and enjoyment,
- promoting teamwork,
- developing individual's skill levels.

Reviews will be different for an individual participant and group participants. The **person responsible** for the activity will lead the review, which may be an **informal or formal** session.

Informal sessions involve a general chat or review games which allow the participants to give feedback on how the session went, both good and bad.

Formal review sessions involve the participants being issued with specific review material such as a formal log book, questionnaires or specialist reviewing materials.

Top Tip
You can learn a lot by working with different coaches, instructors and trainers. They will all have unique reviewing styles!

Reviewing with the person responsible

At the end of the activity session, you will take part in a review of your own performance before, during and after the session. For this review, you may need to bring with you:

- information about the participants,
- activity session plan,
- risk assessment,
- evidence of participant reviews.

The person responsible will usually ask you: how well do you think the session went? Were there aspects of the activity session that you feel need to be improved? Before answering these questions, think about the activity and the participants.

- Did they enjoy the activity?
- Were their aims met?
- Were you able to assist the person responsible during the activity in the way that you had planned?

This information is used to assess whether you were able to carry out the tasks that were planned. **The person responsible will be able to give feedback to you on:**

- your overall performance during the activity session,
- how you performed while explaining and demonstrating aspects of the activity,
- whether the participant's aims were met,
- how you planned and prepared yourself for the session.

Top Tip
Your review of an activity session will be formally recorded as evidence for your assessment.

Quick Test

1 Who will lead the review session for participants?

2 What kind of reviews can you have with participants?

3 When do you review your performance with the person responsible?

4 Name one piece of feedback that the person responsible will give to you.

Answers: **1** The person responsible. **2** Informal and formal. **3** At the end of the activity session. **4** Name any one of the third bulleted list.

What are skills for employment?

The working environment

This Unit is designed to introduce you to what skills you will use in your working environment while under the supervision of the person responsible. This Unit can be integrated with the other four Units in the Skills for Work course – for example, **Facilities and equipment** and **Activity sessions**.

These are clearly split into three distinct areas.

Interacting with customers

In any sport-and-recreation environment you encounter customers all the time. This Unit introduces you to how centres and organisations expect their staff to operate, and to abide by their standards for behaviour (how you conduct yourself) and appearance (wearing a uniform). This Unit will also focus on basic customer interaction and introduce you to communicating with customers, establishing their needs, asking questions, responding to customers' questions where necessary, and good customer care.

Good working relationships with others

This Unit also looks at how you work with others in a realistic working environment. Ideally, it can be integrated with the other Skills for Work Units, as you will be carrying out agreed duties in specified group tasks, therefore you will be maintaining good working relationships with others. It is essential that you ask for help and give assistance to others when it is needed.

Top Tip
You will be working with the person responsible to achieve the desired outcome in this Unit.

Reviewing your performance

This Unit will also focus on how you review your performance with the person responsible. This is done by you collecting feedback on the specified tasks you have carried out. With the person responsible, you will review how well you did and identify any areas that need improvement. Then you will draw up relevant action points to assist you in future activities.

You can achieve the desired outcome of this Unit by:

- assisting with activity sessions,
- carrying out specified tasks and duties around the facility,
- collecting information and reviewing your progress regularly with the person responsible.

What employability skills are in this Unit?

In this Unit you will have the opportunity to develop a range of **employability skills**.

 Reviewing progress/reviewing

 Dealing with customers/customer care

 Taking advice/taking advice from others

 Self-assessment

 Setting targets

 Wearing appropriate dress

 Working cooperatively/working cooperatively with others

T⚙p Tip
Look out for the symbol to see where employability skills have been covered.

T⚙p Tip
Remember, any words in GREEN are explained in the GLOSSARY section on pages 93 and 94.

Occupational standards

Meeting the standards for appearance

Every organisation or centre will have a standard for appearance that all staff must meet. You will find that different organisations and centres will have different standards, and in some cases this can be very strict – for example, you may just be asked to wear the centre's t-shirt and other smart clothing, while in other centres they will supply you with t-shirt, shorts, tracksuit and other uniform.

Whatever the type of uniform the centre asks you to wear, it is important that you wear the uniform that is given to you. Most schools and workplaces require their students/employees to wear clothing that is appropriate to that organisation, but all expect you to look presentable at all times by keeping the uniform clean and tidy!

Examples of different types of standards of appearance are:

School – pupil	Black trousers, white shirt, black jumper, black shoes
Leisure centre – attendant	Company tops (with logo), shorts, trainers
Leisure centre – receptionist	Company tops (with logo), trousers/skirt
Outdoor centre – instructor	Company tops (with logo), trousers

Standards for appearance will also include items of clothing, name badges or jewellery that you can and cannot wear. This is mainly due **to health and safety** issues – for example, if you are taking part in an activity session such as rugby. As rugby is a group activity where a certain amount of contact with others in your team and your opponents is inevitable, items such as jewellery (rings, earrings, necklaces and so on) may get caught or pulled out by accident and will cause the wearer injury.

Top Tip
Make sure you know the standards of appearance for your organisation/ centre.

Behaviour

When you are carrying out your assessments in a realistic working environment, you will be expected to abide by the organisation's/centre's standards of good behaviour at all times.

Each organisation/centre has its own specific policies for how they wish their employees to behave. Most organisations/centres will have the following included in their policies.

- Have an awareness at all times of health and safety relevant to the environment you are in (swimming pool, gym, outdoors etc). This is to ensure that you know how to conduct yourself around activity or leisure sites and venues to prevent you from harming yourself and others.

- Be welcoming and friendly to other colleagues and clients – good customer care is very important to centres and organisations – by treating customers well they will want to return to use the facilities again. Working well with other colleagues is equally important – being friendly enhances your, and their, working environment.

- Do not use **inappropriate language** when in the organisation/centre or when you are in uniform – this will give the centre or organisation you are working for a bad reputation, and you will give a bad impression of yourself to customers, clients and colleagues. Remember: there is a time and a place for everything.

- Abide by the organisation/centre's policies on the use of mobile phones. These policies usually state that while you are on duty in the facility mobile phones must not be used. This also applies when you are assisting activity sessions. However, there are some exceptions to this policy when mobiles are used for safety – activities that take place away from the main centre require a mobile phone to be on hand in case an incident occurs.

Top Tip
Make sure you know your organisation/centre's standards for behaviour.

Quick Test

1 What is the appropriate dress for your school/organisation?

2 Can you give an example of how your uniform/dress should be presentable?

3 Can you name three examples that centres/organisations may include in their policies for behaviour?

1 Candidate to provide answer, eg, black trousers, white shirt, black shoes etc.   2 Clean and tidy.   3 Awareness of health and safety, be welcoming and friendly, do not use inappropriate language, abide by other policies, eg, mobile phone use.

Interacting with customers

Examples

Examples of how customers may interact with you.

- Asking about products or services – customers will come into a centre and need information about the facilities the centre offers.

- Asking about directions within the centre/organisation – this can be the location of an activity or the way to centre facilities, for example, toilets, cafés etc.

- Complaints about services or products – they may ask you how they can place a complaint, or they may inform you that something is not working, such as a broken piece of equipment.

- During activity sessions – by asking questions about an activity, how to demonstrate a particular skill, explaining what you want the participants to do again.

Examples of how you may interact with customers.

- Informing customers of products or services – giving customers information on what the centre does, its facilities and what days activities are running.

- Directing customers away from unsafe areas or situations – these can be the result of broken pieces of equipment or facilities. Unsafe areas could have water on the floor, where customers could slip and hurt themselves, or a fire may require you to assist the person responsible directing customers to the fire assembly point.

- When assisting with activity sessions – communicating what tasks need to be done, and helping with equipping the participants, such as putting on coloured bibs. Interaction can also take place during any explanations and demonstrations you perform in activity sessions.

There are many ways in which we interact with other people. It is very important that, when you are interacting with customers, colleagues and others, you are courteous and polite at all times.

Top Tip
Learn how you can interact well with customers.

Effective communication

Communication is not just about the words you use, but also about the way you speak, write, use body language and, above all, listen. It is important to communicate effectively but also to take into account people's culture and the context in which communication is delivered.

Communication is a two-way process: **listening and talking.**

Listening involves hearing and understanding what is said. Sometimes it can be difficult to hear and understand someone who has a particularly strong accent or dialect. People will sometimes use colloquialisms – this means that they will use a different word for a particular item or thing, for example, 'house' and 'hoose'.

Talking involves thinking what is to be said and verbally conveying the information. When we talk, we have a clear understanding of what we want to say, and we say it. The problem here is that others may not understand what we mean. This could be because what we say may be too difficult for others to understand (consider simplifying words), or we may be talking too fast and, therefore need to slow down – it's not a race, after all! Also take into account that some people may be hard of hearing and therefore may need to see your face to be able to read your lips.

Writing involves thinking what is to be said and writing clearly. This is another way of talking without speaking the words. When we are writing, we have time to think about what it is we need to communicate, and we can also make amendments to the final letter, note and so on. Whatever you are writing, ensure that it says what you want (don't waffle!) and that it can be clearly read by others.

T☼p Tip
Ensure that those receiving your message can understand what you are communicating to them.

✏ Quick Test

1 Give two examples of how customers may interact with you.

2 Give two examples of how you may interact with customers.

3 Name three types of communication.

4 What are the two way processes of communication?

1 About products, services, directions or complaints. 2 Assisting with activity sessions, directing them away from unsafe situations or areas, giving information on products and services. 3 Listening, hearing, writing. 4 Listening and talking.

Communication

Types of communication

Communication is how we interact with others.

Communication is used every day for a variety of reasons, such as exchanging information with customers or colleagues, when attending an interview or when you are just chatting with your friends. There are three main ways in which we communicate:

- **verbal**,
- **written**,
- **body language**.

Verbal communication

Verbal communication is talking.

Examples of verbal communication	How	When
Talking to people	Face to face	Welcoming a customer Communicating with colleagues In a job interview
Using communication devices	Telephones Hand-held radio Intercom	Talking to customers Relaying information to colleagues

Written communication

Written communication is writing or drawing.

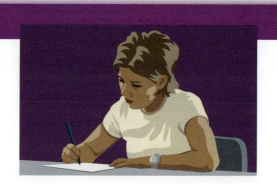

Examples of written communication	How	When
Writing	Notes Memos Letters	Informing colleagues of incidents Passing information onto colleagues who are not on duty at the same time as you
Drawing	Diagrams of facilities Symbols for objects	Carrying out a risk assessment Hazard warning signs

Body language

Types of **body language** are where we unconsciously communicate through the use of postures, gestures or facial expressions.

Posture:

- Sitting in an a chair: a) slumped to one side, resting on the arm of the chair, could mean that you are not interested; b) sitting up, hands on your lap, could mean you are interested in what is going on.

Gesture:

- Putting your hand to your cheek would mean you are thinking about something.
- Tapping or drumming fingers could mean that you are impatient.

Facial expressions:

- Smiling or frowning would give the other person a clear idea what you are thinking. Facial expressions are probably the easiest form of body language to recognise.

Another way in which body language is used for communication is through signing for people who have difficulty hearing. This is called **sign language**.

Below are examples of sign language:

A   B   C

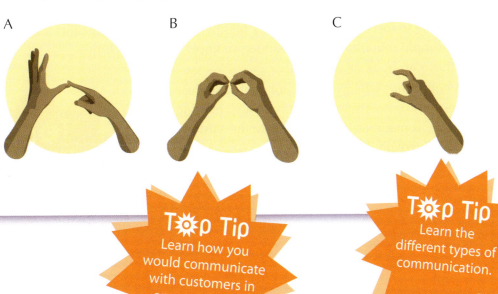

Top Tip
Learn how you would communicate with customers in an organisation or centre.

Top Tip
Learn the different types of communication.

Quick Test

1 Can you name the three most common forms of communication?

2 Identify one method of communicating verbally with customers

3 Identify one method of communicating with customers by written communication.

4 Can you name two forms of body language?

1 Verbal, written, body language. 2 Talking to people or using communication devices. 3 Notes, memos, letters, diagrams or symbols. 4 Posture, gesture or facial expressions.

85

Good customer care

The importance of customer care

Customer care is probably one of the most important of all the skills you will need to develop, especially when you are working with clients. It is important that you give a good impression, as this will **reflect well on the organisation/ centre you work at** or the school you attend.

Every day you will have some customer contact. You may be approached by a customer who requests information about a product or service, or when you are assisting an activity session.

It is important that, no matter what kind of contact you have with customers, you should respond in a number of ways.

- Fairly and quickly – this means a lot to a customer, so don't leave them waiting too long. If you cannot deal with the customer's needs quickly, it is best that you acknowledge that they are there (don't ignore them), and say that you will be with them shortly.

- In a courteous, helpful manner – customers like to be made to feel welcome. Treating them well and be as helpful as you can. Remember that you will not know every answer to every question that a customer asks!

- Listen to the customer's needs and assisting the customer to the best of your ability – by listening to the customer, you may be able to help them yourself. They may have simple requests such as wanting to know where the toilets are, or where they can book an activity.

- Get help from colleagues when you cannot deal with the customer's questions or needs yourself. If you are referring them to another colleague, sometimes it is best to take the customer to this colleague and explain the situation.

Top Tip
Know the main points of good customer care, as you will have to demonstrate them for your assessment.

Relationships with others

In all types of organisations we are in constant contact with other people. These people can be work colleagues, supervisors, managers, school pupils, teachers or others. In some capacity we have a relationship with them, whether this relationship is **professional or as friends**.

In a working environment our relationships with others tend to be more **professional**, and maintaining this can be quite difficult.

Ways of maintaining good working relationships with the people you work with include:

- Turning up on time for work – this will allow you to arrive, dress appropriately for work and sort out your personal belongings into a locker. As a general rule, it is always better to be ten minutes early rather than five minutes late.

- Being courteous and polite to colleagues – behaving in a way that is considerate and polite to colleagues not only makes everyone's day better but also enables everyone to work more effectively.

- Carrying out work duties in line with the organisation/centre's policies for health and safety – this will ensure your safety and make sure that your colleagues are safe, whether you are setting up or taking down equipment or cleaning and tidying the facilities.

- Completing jobs by their specified time – every day you will make a list of all tasks and duties with the person responsible. These tasks will relate to the day and the activities that are booked in, and therefore will have to be done at a certain time and on time. For example, if your task is to assist the person responsible to set up the badminton net by 12:50pm because the activity session begins at 1:00pm, if this does not happen the badminton session will run late, which may have a knock-on effect for other activities for the rest of the day.

Top Tip

Learn how you can maintain good working relationships with others in your centre/organisation.

Quick Test

1 Why must you give a good impression of yourself when dealing with customers?

2 When are you most likely to encounter customers?

3 What kind of relationships could we have with others?

4 What kind of relationships are you most likely to have in a working environment?

1 To reflect well on the organisation/centre you work at. 2 Every day. 3 Professional or as friends. 4 Professional.

Carrying out agreed duties

Tasks

In the Skills for Work course, you will be asked to demonstrate that you can carry out different tasks and duties. These tasks and duties will be discussed with the **person responsible** and then agreed before you begin the work.

Examples of these tasks could be:

- to set up and take down equipment for an activity session,
- ensuring that areas of a facility are clean and tidy,
- preparing a plan for an activity session.

Most centres expect their employees to show proof that daily tasks have been completed – usually via a task sheet. A task sheet may have sections the employee has to sign once the work has been done. Proof of a completed task is also required **for health and safety**. For example, in a swimming-pool environment, the pool water has to be checked at certain times throughout the day/evening when the pool is open. The responsible member of staff will check and test the quality of the pool water, note their findings in a report and sign it off.

Top Tip

When tasks are set for you, make sure that you and the person responsible have signed them off when they have been completed. This evidence is used for your assessment.

Giving assistance

When approached by someone who requires your assistance, try to be **courteous and show willingness to help**. There are many different situations where you may find yourself helping others to carry out activities, this can include tasks such as:

- setting up, taking down and storing equipment,
- equipping clients for activities,
- during accidents and emergencies,
- when dealing with customer needs.

However, there may be occasions when you are unable to assist others – for example, when **you have not been trained for the task or when the assistance is beyond your level of responsibility**. If this is the case, then politely tell the person your reasons and perhaps suggest someone else.

Asking for assistance

When asking others for help, it is important to consider:

- how you ask,
- what it is you want them to do,
- that you should not be upset if they are unable to help you!

T☀p Tip

Can you give examples where you have given assistance to others and asked for help? This information is useful when you carry out your review with the person responsible.

✎ Quick Test

1 Who will tasks and duties be agreed with before you begin any work or activity?

2 Give one example why proof of a task has to be completed.

3 When you are approached by someone, what must you try to be?

4 Give an example of a situation where you may not be able to assist others.

1 The person responsible. **2** For health and safety. **3** Courteous and show willingness to help. **4** When you have not been trained for the task or when the assistance is beyond your level of responsibility.

Gathering feedback

Methods

Feedback can be gathered in a number of ways.

- Take part in reviews or evaluations of your work. These can be formal (meetings) or informal (verbal feedback).
- Use the Employability Skills Review sheet.
- Gather statements from colleagues or from the person responsible on the work you have carried out.

The feedback you gather can be from your performance training assisting with activities, from your personal fitness training and so on. This information is then used to form the basis of a more **formal review session**. With the person responsible, you will identify your strengths, weaknesses and areas for improvement, and agree action points.

Identifying strengths and weaknesses

At set points during this Skills for Work course you will take part in reviews of the work and training sessions you have taken part in.

These reviews are designed to focus on all aspects of **your course and your learning**, in particular your interactions with customers and maintaining relationships with others. Thinking about these relationships will help you to identify your **strengths and weaknesses**.

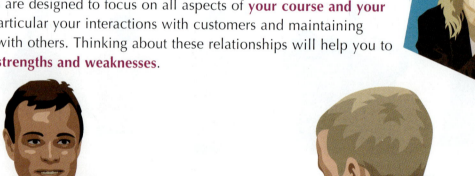

What are my strengths?
- *Communicating with customers*

What are my weaknesses?
- *Wearing the correct protective equipment*

Action points:
- *Before starting a task or activity, find out what equipment is needed.*
- *Try to be ten minutes early at the centre in the mornings.*
- *Work with different people who are taking activities to gain reviewing experience.*

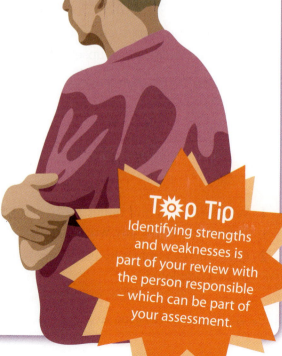

Top Tip
Identifying strengths and weaknesses is part of your review with the person responsible – which can be part of your assessment.

Improvement and action

Once you have identified the skills you need to improve, you may need to put them in order of importance depending on what activities you are taking part in. The person responsible will list **action points**, for example:

Activities	Areas for improvement
Tidying up areas in a facility	Time keeping Wearing protective equipment
Assisting with activity sessions	Dressing appropriately Giving feedback to the clients
All activities	Timekeeping – being on time in the morning

What are my strengths?
- Communicating with customers

What are my weaknesses?
- Wearing the correct protective equipment

Action points:
- Before starting a task or activity, find out what equipment is needed.
- Try to be ten minutes early at the centre in the mornings.
- Work with different people who are taking activities to gain reviewing experience.

Top Tip
Identifying action points gives you something to focus on when trying to improve.

 Quick Test

1 How can the information you gather from others be used?

2 What are reviews designed to focus on?

3 What is the first thing you should identify during your review?

4 After identifying the areas you need to improve on, what does the person responsible list?

Glossary

Absorbed Here the body has taken in the substance through the skin.

Accident Something that can happen unexpectedly at any time that has the potential to cause harm, e.g., grazed knee, cut finger etc.

Confidential Information which is private to individuals and cannot be made public without the individual giving consent.

Constructive To improve or promote development – balancing up negative comments with positive alternatives.

COSHH Control of Substances Hazardous to Health – a set of regulations to ensure the safety of people who have to deal with substances e.g. chemicals.

Data Protection Act (1998) This act ensures that companies comply with the regulation of information held, obtained or disclosed about individuals.

Duty of care This is a legal obligation imposed on an individual requiring that they exercise a reasonable standard of care while performing any acts that could potentially harm others. Also a legal obligation that centres have over their employees/staff.

EAP Emergency Action Plan – a document that informs staff of what to do when an emergency takes place, ie. fire, accident.

Emergency An unforeseen incident that needs immediate action, e.g., fire, theft.

Employability skills Skills you must demonstrate in order to pass the course. See page 9 for a list of all the employability skills.

Hazard A hazard is anything with the potential to cause harm e.g. water on a floor.

Hazardous substances Substances can be solid, liquid or gas. If they enter your body they can cause you harm.

Health and safety A set of rules and regulations that all centres, staff and users must abide by to ensure their safety.

Inappropriate language Words or phases that you should not use in the centre, especially when talking to customers and participants, ie. swearing.

Induction A formal process where new members of staff or clients are shown around a centre. Health, safety and emergency facilities are included in an induction.

Ingested Where the body has swallowed a substance.

Inhaled Where the body has breathed in a substance.

Injected Where the body has taken in a substance directly e.g. through a needle.

Manual Handling Operations Regulations A set of regulations to ensure that companies train their staff in the correct ways to lift, lower, pull and push large, heavy and awkward objects, in order to minimise injury to staff and clients.

Medical assistance A person who is trained medially and can give advanced care to casualties, e.g. doctor, paramedic, nurse.

NABS National Assessment Banks – your assessment paperwork.

Negligence is a failure to act on an occurance that subsequently has a damaging effect on others. A negligence suit is a form of legal action where it is proved or disproved that negligence took place and that someone or an organisation was responsible for a breach of duty of care.

NOP Normal Operating Plan – these documents outline how a centre operates safely for its users and staff.

Person responsible The person who has direct responsibility for you e.g. teacher, tutor, instructor, coach, assessor, trainer.

PPE Personal Protective Equipment – the correct and relevant equipment that must be worn when carrying out certain tasks ie. first-aid, cleaning and tidying.

Realistic working environment The place where you will carry out your assessments. For example, these facilities can be leisure centres, fitness suites or outdoor centres.

Reports Reports are an account of something that has happened. Reports are a centre requirement. Most incidents require a written report, such as an accident report form.

Risk assessment Careful examination of what could cause harm to people in any given situation. This process enables you to identify whether you have taken enough precautions or should do more to prevent harm to yourself or others using the facility.

Scenarios Small role play situations that you will have to act out in a sport and recreation environment.

Triage A term used in an accident situation when you have to decide which casualty receives treatment first.

Unconscious When a casualty is not responding to you in any form. Levels of unconsciousness are determined by AVPU (see page 36).

Unit Specifications A document that contains information about what you have to do in order to pass your course.

Index